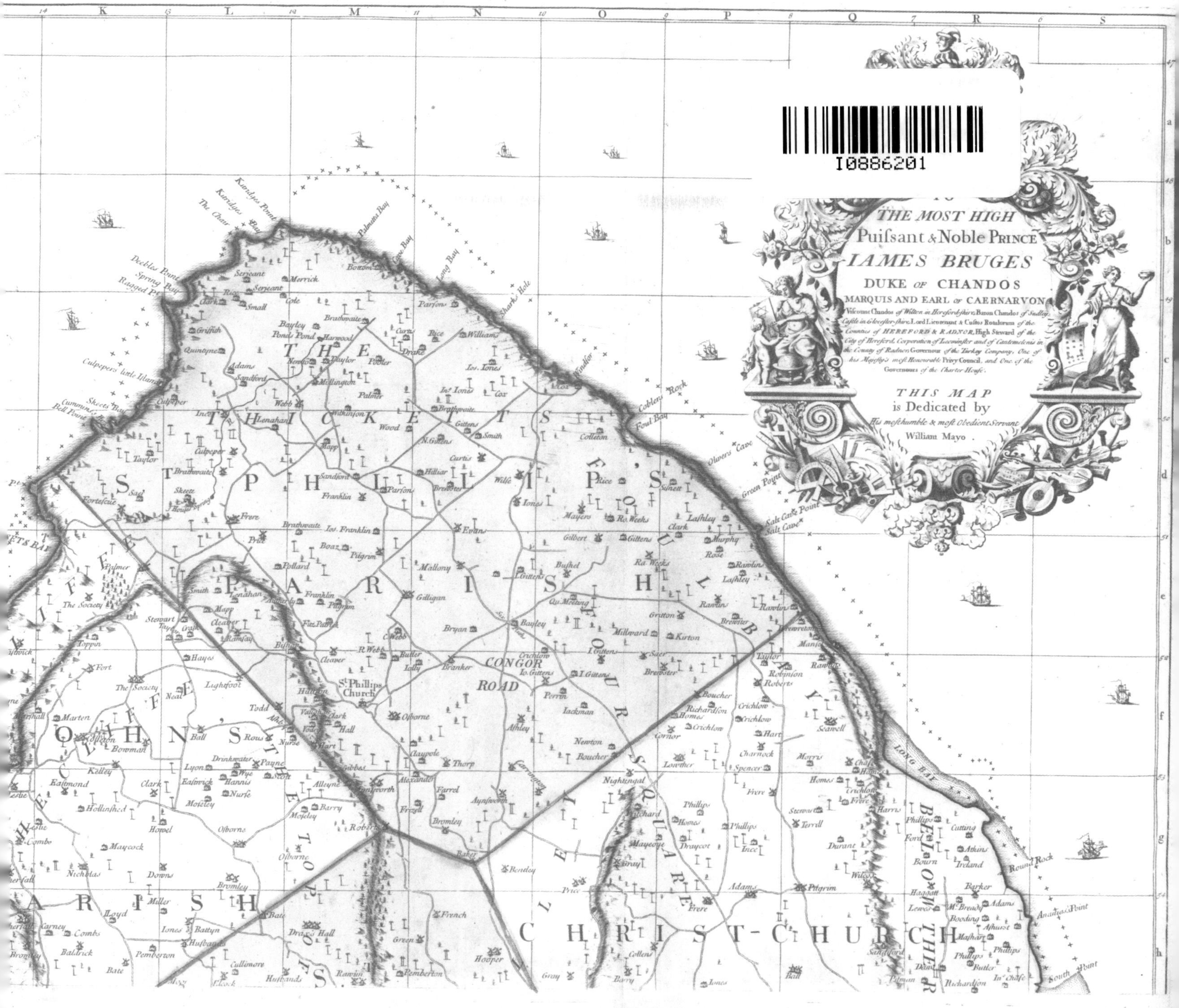
THE MOST HIGH
Puissant & Noble Prince
JAMES BRUGES
DUKE OF CHANDOS
MARQUIS AND EARL OF CAERNARVON
THIS MAP
is Dedicated by
His most humble & most Obedient Servant
William Mayo.
ST PHILLIPS PARISH
THE THICKETS
CONGOR ROAD
St. Phillips Church
CHRIST-CHURCH
LONG BAY
Round Rock
Coblers Rock
Foul Bay
Olivers Cave
Green Point
Salt Cave Point
Salt Cave
Palmeto Bay
Long Bay
Sharks Hole
Kendals Point
Culpepers little Iland
Skeets Bay
Spring Bay
Ragged Pt.
Anatias Point
South Point

GEORGE WASHINGTON'S BARBADOS DIARY

1751–52

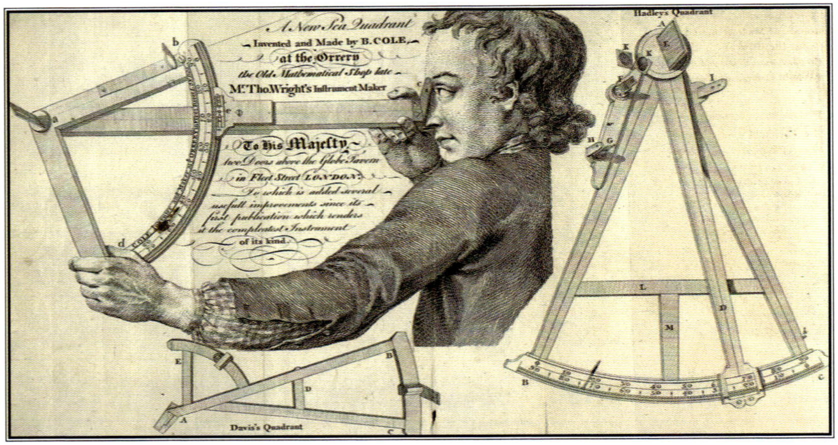
A New Sea Quadrant
Invented and Made by B. COLE,
at the Orrery
the Old Mathematical Shop late
Mr. Tho. Wright's Instrument Maker
To His Majesty
two Doors above the Globe Tavern
in Fleet Street LONDON.
To which is added several
usefull improvements since its
first publication which renders
it the compleatest Instrument
of its kind.
Hadley's Quadrant
Davis's Quadrant

GEORGE WASHINGTON'S BARBADOS DIARY

1751–52

ALICIA K. ANDERSON & LYNN A. PRICE

Editors

WILLIAM M. FERRARO

Editor in Chief

UNIVERSITY OF VIRGINIA PRESS

Charlottesville & London

This edition has been prepared by the staff of

THE WASHINGTON PAPERS

sponsored by

The Mount Vernon Ladies' Association of the Union
and the University of Virginia.

UNIVERSITY OF VIRGINIA PRESS

Printed in Canada

First published 2018

The paper used in this publication meets the minimum requirements of
ANSI/NISO Z39.48–1992 (R 1997) (Permanence of Paper).

Library of Congress Cataloging-in-Publication Data
Washington, George, 1732–1799.
Names: Washington, George, 1732–1799. | Anderson, Alicia K., editor. | Price, Lynn A., editor. | Ferraro, William M., editor.
Title: George Washington's Barbados diary, 1751–52 / Alicia K. Anderson and
Lynn A. Price, Editors ; William M. Ferraro, Editor in Chief.
Description: Charlottesville : UNIVERSITY OF VIRGINIA PRESS, 2018. | "This edition has been prepared by the staff of The Washington Papers, sponsored by The Mount Vernon Ladies' Association of the Union and the University of Virginia." | Includes bibliographical references and index.
Identifiers: LCCN 2018002830 | ISBN 9780813941370 (cloth : alk. paper)
Subjects: LCSH: Washington, George, 1732–1799—Diaries. | Barbados—Description and travel—Early works to 1800.
Classification: LCC E312.8 2018 | DDC 973.4/1092—dc23
LC record available at https://lccn.loc.gov/2018002830

FRONT AND BACK ENDPAPERS

A New & Exact Map of the Island of Barbadoes in America According to an Actual & Accurate Survey Made in the Years 1717 and 1721 . . . by William Mayo, 1722. (Courtesy of John Carter Brown Library)

FRONTISPIECE

Hadley's Quadrant, also known as Hadley's octant, in Benjamin Cole, *The Description and Use of a New Quadrant, For Finding the Latitude at Sea*, 2nd ed., London, 1749. (Courtesy of British Library)

This publication was made possible thanks to the generous support of:

Geraldine W. Dellenback in Memory of Robert J. Dellenback

Life Guard Society for Historic Mount Vernon

Mount Vernon Ladies' Association of the Union

CONTENTS

ILLUSTRATIONS

MAPS

GEORGE WASHINGTON'S
BARBADOS DIARY

1751–52

FOREWORD

In the fall of 1751, nineteen-year-old George Washington went on a sea voyage from Virginia to Bridgetown, Barbados. He accompanied his older half brother Maj. Lawrence Washington, who was traveling in an ultimately vain hope to improve his health. It was a voyage to remember: the first time Washington sailed on the open sea, his first trip to another British colony, likely the first time he saw a professional theater performance, and the first (and only) time he got smallpox. Thankfully for posterity, George Washington kept a record of his trip.

This definitive edition of George Washington's journal of his voyage to Barbados is the first to appear in more than one hundred years, and it represents the finest edition ever produced. Every historian who seriously attempts to write about the early life of George Washington will need to reference and read this version. Readers will find the notoriously challenging journal—now enhanced with annotations, a scholarly introduction, and four appendices—to be a useful glimpse into a slice of Washington's often romanticized early years. As there are no other letters from this period of his life, the journal provides an essential and tangible bridge to help piece together the arc of his story and his times in the years immediately before he began a public career that would ultimately be of so much consequence—for his own fame, for the future of the United States, and for the world.

At sea from September to November, the Washingtons made landfall in the British colony on 2 Nov. 1751. The trip was filled with wonders for Washington. He was already familiar with measuring and describing the land as a surveyor, and Washington's journal shows that he eagerly learned the conventions and vicissitudes of the sea as he attempted to track the ship's place in the ocean, with regular measurements of the wind, the declination of the sun, records of other ships observed in transit, and a thorough log of the weather. While Barbados and Virginia shared the distinction of being among the oldest British dominions in the Atlantic Empire, these colonies seemed quite distinct to the young George Washington. The climate, the landscape, the sugar crop, the fashion, the social structure, even the accents of the locals, all spoke to him of an exotic, distinctive culture. He brought a youthful enthusiasm to his descriptions of the "beautiful prospects" of Barbados, but he also revealed that keen eye for the strategic and military disposition of the island, which foreshadows his future career.

The trip also served a crucial business purpose. The two Washington brothers would meet the extended family and commercial network of the Fairfaxes, who were Lawrence's in-laws and neighbors at Mount Vernon. They likely sailed on a ship owned by Alexandria merchant John Carlyle—a fact discovered by the editors of this edition—who also married a Fairfax daughter and thus made up a crucial pillar of the Fairfax "interest" in northern Virginia. George Washington would climb these connections to fame and influence. He was a Briton in 1751, and his exposure to the greater British world would serve him well.

Scholars, students, and general readers will find this little edition an excellent example of the power of professional editing, brimming with insights into a world now lost. The Mount Vernon Ladies' Association of the Union (MVLA), which sponsored the creation of this book, is delighted to help enhance the ability of future historians and readers to recover the context and drama of the story of America's most important Founding Father. Since 1968 the MVLA has been a leading supporter of the project to transcribe and annotate all of the papers of George Washington. With the opening in 2013 of the Fred W. Smith National Library for the Study of George Washington, the MVLA initiated a series of efforts to increase that support and encourage the creation of more scholarship to map the full context of the life and legacy of George Washington. In addition to hiring a full-time editor for the ongoing Papers of George Washington, the MVLA sponsored "The Washington Family Papers" project, an effort to transcribe and annotate the papers of Martha Washington and those of George Washington's parents and near relations, including Bushrod Washington, the nephew who would inherit Mount Vernon. This complete transcription of the Barbados diary, with accompanying commentary, represents the first publication in the Washington Family Papers Project. It is an excellent beginning.

DOUGLAS BRADBURN
President and CEO
George Washington's Mount Vernon
Mount Vernon, Virginia, April 25, 2018

ACKNOWLEDGMENTS

The editors gratefully acknowledge the many contributions vital to publishing this edition of the Barbados diary. First and foremost, the Mount Vernon Ladies' Association of the Union made this project possible through a generous grant. Critical support also came from the Fred W. Smith National Library for the Study of George Washington, and in particular from founding director Douglas Bradburn, research historian Mary V. Thompson, former Special Collections librarian Michele Lee, former Access Services librarian Sarah Myers, and manager of Visual Resources Dawn Bonner.

The generosity and kindness of local professionals facilitated on-location research of Barbados history and George Washington. The editors specifically thank noted historian Karl Watson, who gave his time to take us on a tour of relevant sites around the island. Martin Miller, an interpreter at the George Washington House, provided indispensable context. The editors are also grateful to the Barbados Department of Archives and the Barbados Museum and Historical Society for use of their research collections.

The Library of Congress holds the original manuscript of the Barbados diary. The editors thank the Manuscript Division, and particularly historian Julie Miller, for allowing us to examine the manuscript. Yasmeen Khan, a senior conservator at the Library of Congress, usefully explained the history of the diary as an object.

Roughly half of Washington's Barbados voyage account involves seafaring. Personnel at the Naval History and Heritage Command who generously contributed expert advice include senior historian Michael Crawford, historian and documentary histories technical lead Dennis M. Conrad, and historian Peter Luebke. In addition, we thank maritime archaeologist Jason Lunze for sharing his sweeping knowledge of eighteenth-century vessels, sailing, and the Atlantic world economy.

Lawrence Thomas, professor emeritus of mathematics at the University of Virginia, and Christina Osborne, graduate student in mathematics at the university, carefully reviewed the calculations used to reconstruct the data within the ship's log.

Also among those who provided invaluable assistance to the editors are anthropologist and Barbados scholar Jerome S. Handler, historical archaeologist Philip Levy, and historian Andrew Jackson O'Shaughnessy.

Finally, colleagues at The Washington Papers gave significant time and expertise. Particular contributions came from Kathryn Blizzard, Kim Curtis, Thomas E. Dulan, William M. Ferraro, Kathryn Gehred, Jane Haxby, and Mary K. Wigge. Cartographer Rick Britton offered creative solutions as we collaborated on the new maps in this volume. Advice from Mark Saunders, Mark Mones, Anne Hegeman, and Cecilia Sorochin at the University of Virginia Press guided some decisions on content and presentation.

The editors, of course, remain responsible for any oversights or errors in the volume.

A HISTORY OF PUBLISHED EDITIONS OF THE BARBADOS DIARY

Despite the editorial attention lavished on George Washington's documentary record since his death in 1799, no full and satisfying rendering exists of the diary he kept during his voyage to Barbados between the fall of 1751 and winter of 1752. Supreme Court Chief Justice John Marshall, given complete access to Washington's papers to produce the first multivolume biography, simply ignored the Barbados trip.[1] The paucity of surviving documentary material on Washington's early adulthood argues forcibly for a comprehensive and authoritative edition—one that avoids the weaknesses and builds on the strengths of earlier efforts.[2]

Jared Sparks (1789–1866)

Barbados diary entries appeared in print for the first time in the appendix to the second volume of Jared Sparks's *The Writings of George Washington* (Boston, 1833–37). In a section entitled "Washington's Early Papers," Sparks supplied a "few short extracts" from papers then at Mount Vernon, "fragments of manuscripts written by Washington during his boyhood and youth." Selections from the Barbados diary span Washington's stay on the island, beginning with a welcome on 3 Nov. 1751 and concluding with his reflections on island life and culture upon his departure seven weeks later.[3]

Sparks scoured archives across America and Europe to find and publish manuscripts from the founding era of the United States. Among the works of this ordained Unitarian minister and Harvard College president are extensive editions of the papers of Benjamin Franklin and Gouverneur Morris. He published twelve volumes of Washington's *Writings* and four volumes of his incoming letters, entitled *Correspondence of the American Revolution* (Boston, 1853). At his death, an obituary lauded Sparks for his "thorough research, candid judgment, dispassionate criticism, and accuracy and simplicity of style."[4]

Sparks, however, drew criticism for not printing entire documents.[5] Choosing from the Barbados diary only what he deemed "not . . . uninteresting," he omitted the ship's log, the entries from the return voyage, and the fragmentary items following Washington's arrival in Virginia.[6] Sparks did publish the entries for 3 and 4 Nov. 1751, which can be found nowhere else. He also published significant portions of two now-missing letters from Lawrence Washington—one from Barbados and one from Bermuda (see Appendix C).

Sparks's transcription policy presents obvious problems. He altered, added, or omitted words and phrases to reflect what he considered proper usage or Washington's true intent. The approach misrepresents young George's spelling and occasional awkward phrasing. The rushed tone of quickly written entries also is lost. In the diary entry for 4 Nov., Sparks quoted Washington as being "perfectly enraptured with the beautiful prospects," when he actually wrote that he was "ravished" by the prospects. In the entry for 12 Dec., Sparks truncated the name of a man on trial to "Colonel C.," while it is spelled out in the manuscript as "Chaunack." Sparks also demonstrated inappropriate delicacy when he deleted the observation that Chaunack "was indicted for commiting a rape on his servant Maid."[7] Sparks argued that his duty called for such a transcription policy, but criticism has persisted over the years.[8]

Along with purposeful alterations, Sparks committed transcription blunders. He read "singular risings" rather than "regular risings" in the description of the Barbados landscape. When Washington discussed the sugar industry and estimated that a third of the land was "in Cane for Harvest," Sparks rendered "in train for harvest."[9] And by not noting the days of the week as written in the diary, Sparks failed to realize that Washington misdated several entries.[10] In brief, the Sparks version of the Barbados diary exhibits many shortcomings.

Joseph M. Toner (1825–1896)

Joseph Meredith Toner, an eminent Washington, D.C., medical doctor, antiquarian, and public benefactor, published the first and only complete transcription of the Barbados diary in 1892. After graduating from Philadelphia's Jefferson Medical College in 1853, Toner practiced general medicine in the nation's capital and led many professional organizations over the next four decades. He also actively collected and researched historical documents. In 1882 he donated his immense personal library to the Library of Congress, where it still resides.[11]

Toner built a reputation as the "first authority" on Washington's private life.[12] "There was certainly no man as familiar as he with the daily life of the first President," observed the writer of his obituary in the (Washington) *Evening Star*, reflecting that it had been Toner's "aim to make a complete collection of Washington's letters and writing of every sort, a task that no one else had ever attempted."[13] He focused on Washington's early diaries and writings, most notably publishing his *Journal of My Journey Over the Mountains . . . While Surveying for Lord Thomas Fairfax . . . in 1747–8* (Albany, N.Y., 1892) and "Washington in the Forbes Expedition of 1758" in volume 1 of the *Records of the Columbia Historical Society* (1897, pp. 185–213). A "lifelong student and investigator," Toner earned praise for being "precise and thorough to the last degree."[14]

Toner published *The Daily Journal of Major George Washington, in 1751–2, Kept while on a Tour from Virginia to the Island of Barbadoes, with his invalid Brother, Maj. Lawrence Washington, Proprietor of Mount Vernon on the Potomac* (Albany, N.Y., 1892), after thoroughly examining the original manuscript. That volume, now available at about one hundred and fifty libraries worldwide, mimics the look of the manuscript diary more than any other edition. The printing company Joel Munsell's Sons, founded around 1828 with a focus on history books, published the volume in a small print run of no more than a few hundred copies.[15] A year later, James H. Stark reprinted Washington's island entries from Toner's text, crediting the publisher rather than the editor for putting the manuscript "within the reach of all."[16]

Unlike Sparks, Toner strove for completeness and "literal exactness," noting that "I have had copied every letter, word and sentence of the Journal from beginning to end which can be deciphered" and asserting, "I hazard but little in saying that no future copyist will ever be able to make out more or as much of the Journal as this transcript contains."[17] Toner's care in dealing with the text resulted in readings from the manuscript that later damage rendered impossible. An example is the inclusion of "Beef" on the Christmas menu aboard the ship sailing home; another instance is Washington's meeting "Majr. Dan< >" in Virginia (see the entries for 25 Dec. 1751 and 3 Feb. 1752). Toner's transcription does contain flaws. He misread as numbers the abbreviations for "observation" in the ship's log (see the entries for 21–23 Oct.).[18] In the entry for 5 Nov., Guy Fawkes Day, Toner rendered "bring guns &." instead of "being Gun P[owder] T[reason]."[19] Despite the numerous strengths and fewer shortcomings of Toner's edition, nearly all Washington scholars and biographers have overlooked it, with Barbados historian Karl Watson being an exception.[20]

John C. Fitzpatrick (1876–1940)

John Clement Fitzpatrick left his mark as an editor of Washington's papers in the early twentieth century. As assistant chief of the Division of Manuscripts at the Library of Congress for almost thirty years, he influenced how archivists cared for and studied paper records. But he considered the study of Washington to be his "life work."[21] He calendared the vast holdings of Washington's documents in the Library of Congress and prepared books and articles about the man and his times. With assistance from the Mount Vernon Ladies' Association of the Union, Fitzpatrick in 1925 published the four-volume *Diaries of George Washington, 1748–1799*. Under the auspices of the United States George Washington Bicentennial Commission, he subsequently edited *The Writings of George Washington from the Original Manuscript Sources, 1745–1799*, which would span thirty-nine volumes from 1931 to 1944. "The cumulative effect of his work as editor," an obituary claimed, "was to make him the foremost authority on the personal life and the writings of Washington."[22]

In the first volume of *Diaries*, Fitzpatrick adeptly skirted the problems posed by physical damage to the Barbados diary. Departing from Toner, who specifically described or re-created the appearance of the mutilated passages, Fitzpatrick used ellipses to represent missing text cleanly and concisely. Starting with 4 Oct. 1751, which he deemed "the first unmutilated entry," Fitzpatrick reproduced all narrative text to the last surviving entries in early February 1752. Although much more inclusive than Sparks, Fitzpatrick omitted material Toner had included, because he chose to print only "that portion [of the diary] that makes sense and conveys information." Most significantly, Fitzpatrick dismissed the mathematical records tracking the ship's position on the voyage to Barbados as "difficult to reproduce in type and of no value to the diary record."[23] He also refused to reprint material found only in the Sparks edition, citing his predecessor's "well-known method of taking liberties with Washington's composition."[24]

Contemporary reviewers praised Fitzpatrick's edition of the diaries. "The editing leaves little to be desired," observed noted diplomatic historian Samuel Flagg Bemis.[25] "The editorial work has been accomplished with success, reserve, and discretion," proclaimed Archibald Henderson, who stood in awe of the quantity of new material first printed in the edition, going on to note that "Mr. Fitzpatrick has been fortunate in having access to the exhaustive investigations of the late J. M. Toner, an indefatigable and zealous student of the materials of the diaries."[26] Fitzpatrick's edition became the favorite of twentieth-century Washington scholars, among them Rupert Hughes, Bernard Faÿ, Walter H. Mazyck, Charles H. Ambler, Douglas Southall Freeman, Bernhard Knollenberg, James Thomas Flexner, and Ralph K. Andrist.[27] Andrew Jackson O'Shaughnessy and Matthew Mulcahy, modern historians of the Caribbean, still prefer Fitzpatrick's text.[28]

In the first volume of his edition of Washington's *Writings*, Fitzpatrick selected very few entries from the Barbados diary, including only those on Washington's bout with smallpox, his return voyage to Virginia, and his meeting with Gov. Robert Dinwiddie, and identifying these extracts as "the only ones of prime importance in the journal in relation to George Washington."[29] A reviewer attacked Fitzpatrick for his decision.[30]

Donald Jackson (1919–1987) and Dorothy Twohig (1927–2011)

Donald Jackson, professor of history at the University of Virginia, served as the first editor in chief of The Papers of George Washington, from its inception in 1968 to his retirement in 1977. Previously editor and associate director of the University of Illinois Press, Jackson wrote or edited numerous biographical and historical works, most notably titles on the American West.[31] Dorothy Twohig, formerly an editor with The Papers of Alexander Hamilton, joined Jackson as associate editor and remained with The Papers of George Washington for almost thirty years, serving as editor in chief from 1992 to 1998.[32] Jackson and Twohig coedited the project's first series, the six-volume *Diaries of George Washington* (Charlottesville, Va., 1976–79). The first volume featured a facsimile of the Barbados diary manuscript with extensive editorial commentary.

Jackson's correspondence with Mount Vernon librarian Frank E. Morse in 1971 suggests initial plans to publish a transcription of the diary. "And as for Toner," reported Jackson, "we use only his transcripts—and then only to corroborate our own guesses in transcribing a mutilated or faded diary."[33] For reasons that remain unclear, Jackson and Twohig decided not to publish their transcription, which remains among the project's archives.

The publication of a facsimile edition rather than a full transcription fueled criticism. "The only questionable editorial decision, at least for this reviewer," wrote Lowell H. Harrison, professor of history at Western Kentucky University, "is the inclusion of seventy-nine facsimile pages of Washington's 1751–1752 journey to Barbados. If the editors could not decipher the deteriorated manuscript, readers are not likely to do better."[34] A more sympathetic reviewer found the decision to print the diary in facsimile understandable, as transcription would pose "serious typographical problems." Without benefit of a transcript, however, casual readers "may quickly give up the attempt to read the handwriting of the youthful Washington." Placing annotation before the manuscript only increased "the reader's difficulties."[35] In his 2015 biography of George Washington, noted historian Robert Middlekauff bluntly dismissed the facsimile edition as "not useful."[36]

Twohig revisited the Barbados diary in *George Washington's Diaries: An Abridgment* (Charlottesville, Va., 1999).[37] Her transcription presents only extracts from the island visit, but popular historians have used the selections.[38]

The Current Edition

Evaluations of every previous treatment inform this new edition of the Barbados diary. The editors also have studied the manuscript before and after a 1987 restoration, employing the 1964 microfilm (now digitized) and digital photographs taken during their visit to the Library of Congress in 2015. The clarity and magnification of the recent digital images have made possible more-accurate transcriptions. Besides what can be read from the manuscript, renderings preserved in Toner's *Daily Journal* and Fitzpatrick's *Diaries* have been incorporated into the text with explanatory notes.

Extensive new analysis and research have improved the published text. Ship's log data that was lost to mutilation has been reconstructed through careful mathematical calculations of the geographic coordinates for the entire voyage to Barbados. A new visualization of the ship's course based on these coordinates also reveals the substantial error found in Washington's own records (see the map entitled "A Voyage to Barbados, 1751" and Appendix B). Primary sources located only in Barbadian archives augment several identifications. Informed by these developments, the letterpress and digital editions will make a definitive version of the Barbados diary accessible to readers for years to come.

The Manuscript

Although it survives tenuously in severely mutilated condition, the diary remains exceptional because it reveals a youthful George Washington. Sparks, who observed the document in the 1830s, lamented that "time and accident have made such breaches in the manuscript, that little can now be gathered from it."[39] Toner remarked in the 1890s that the first part of the diary was "so fragmentary as to be practically unintelligible," and observed that "the paper has lost its strength and tenacity, breaking on the least handling, and has already, to a considerable extent, crumbled into dust. Page after page has already disappeared from the volume, a fringe of many leaves, only, remaining along the back where it is sewed."[40] Fitzpatrick assessed all Washington's diaries and described the Barbados manuscript as "the worst mutilated of all the surviving originals."[41]

In its present state, the manuscript is a booklet of eighty-four pages (forty-two double-sided leaves numbered from "2" to "43") with blank cover pages. The internal pages are octavo size, meaning that the original leaves were folded three times; the cover pages are formed from a folded quarto sheet twice the size of the interior leaves. Multiple conservation attempts have left their marks on the document. The U.S. Department of State purchased this and Washington's other early diaries from his grandnephew George Corbin Washington in 1849. Late in the nineteenth century, as the State Department was restoring, mounting, and binding other Washington manuscripts, the diary was disassembled and its pages were numbered. Following its subsequent transfer to the Library of Congress in 1904, it was conserved through the process of silking, a state-of-the-art technique at the time that involved pasting a layer of gauze over manuscript pages, which in the case of the diary led to slight blurring and fading of the ink. The library released a microfilm shot from the silked version in 1964 and has since made the film image available digitally.

A sophisticated reconservation was performed in 1987, during which the silking was removed through enzyme baths and each page was leaf cast—carefully repaired with paper pulp—before being rebound into a slender volume. The diary is thus a cohesive whole, with its contents divided for the purposes of this edition into four parts—the voyage to Barbados, the stay on the island, the return voyage, and Washington's arrival in Virginia—for ease of interpretation and presentation.

---

1. See John Marshall, *The Life of George Washington, Commander in Chief of the American Forces, during the War which established the Independence of His Country, and First President of the United States* (5 vols., 1804–7; reprint, 2 vols., Philadelphia, 1850).

2. For an assessment of GW biographies that buttresses this contention, see Philip Levy, *George Washington Written Upon the Land: Nature, Memory, Myth, & Landscape* (Morgantown, W.V., 2015), 1–58.

3. Sparks, *Writings*, 2:411, 424–27.

4. *New York Herald* for 15 March 1866; see also Herbert B. Adams, *The Life and Writings of Jared Sparks: Comprising Selections from His Journals and Correspondence* (2 vols.; Boston and New York, 1893).

5. For a vigorous response to his critics, see Sparks, *A Reply to the Strictures of Lord Mahon and Others, on the Mode of Editing the Writings of Washington* (Cambridge, Mass., 1852), and *Letter to Lord Mahon, Being an Answer to His Letter Addressed to the Editor of Washington's Writings* (Boston, 1852).

6. Sparks, *Writings*, 2:424.

7. For these passages in Sparks, see *Writings*, 2:424–25.

8. See, particularly, the reviews of Sparks, *Writings*, in *North American Review* 39 (1834): 467–94, and by Wayne E. Stevens in *MVHR* 20 (1933–34): 410–11.

9. GW's entry for 22 Dec., and Sparks, *Writings*, 2:425–26.

10. See the entry for 3 Nov., n.1.

11. See *Evening Star* (Washington, D.C.) for 26 May 1894 and 1 Aug. 1896; *Sun* (Baltimore) for 3 Aug. 1896; and "Joseph Meredith Toner, M.D., Ph.D.," *Records of The Columbia Historical Society* 48–49 (1949): 350–52.

12. *Evening Star* (Washington, D.C.) for 26 May 1894.

13. *Evening Star* (Washington, D.C.) for 1 Aug. 1896.

14. Ibid. For more about Toner's publishing aspirations and achievements, see *DGW* 1:xlvii–xlviii.

15. See Peter R. Eisenstadt and Laura-Eve Moss, comps., *The Encyclopedia of New York State* (Syracuse, N.Y., 2005), 1266, and Henry S. Bannister, "From the Collector's Library: Joel Munsell, Printer and Antiquarian in Albany, New York," *Courier* 11 (1974): 11–22. See also *DGW* 1:xlviii.

16. James H. Stark, *Stark's History and Guide to Barbados and the Caribbee Islands, containing a description of everything on or about these islands of which the visitor or resident may desire information, including their History, Inhabitants, Climate, Agriculture, Geology, Government and Resources* (Boston and Barbados, 1893), 185.

17. Toner, *Daily Journal*, 7–8.

18. Toner read "ob." as "06" (*Daily Journal*, 32–33).

19. Toner, *Daily Journal*, 46.

20. See Watson, *Civilised Island, Barbados*, 42; Smith and Watson, "Urbanity, Sociability, and Commercial Exchange in the Barbados Sugar Trade," 71, 79.

For other investigators who consulted Toner's edition, see Knollenberg, *Washington: The Virginia Period,* 144, and Carey, "Inventing Caribbean Climates," 136.

21. *American Historical Review* 45 (1939–40): 1005.

22. Ibid.

23. Fitzpatrick, *Diaries*, 1:16–17.

24. Ibid., 1:22. In taking the transcription from Toner's edition for the 4 Nov. entry, however, Fitzpatrick failed to notice that Toner's text came from Sparks.

25. *American Historical Review* 31 (1925–26): 543. See also Evarts B. Greene's review in *Political Science Quarterly* 41 (1926): 292.

26. *North Carolina Historical Review* 3 (1926): 375.

27. See R. Hughes, *Washington*, 58–64, 509; Faÿ, *Washington*, 46–48; Mazyck, *Washington and the Negro*, 3–4; Ambler, *Washington and the West*, 26; Freeman, *Washington*, 1:247–58; Knollenberg, *Washington: The Virginia Period*, 8–9, 119; Flexner, *Washington*, 49–51, 60; and Andrist, *Founding Fathers: Washington*, 27–28.

28. See Andrew Jackson O'Shaughnessy, *An Empire Divided: The American Revolution and the British Caribbean* (Philadelphia, 2000), 10, 27, 48; and Matthew Mulcahy, *Hubs of Empire: The Southeastern Lowcountry and British Caribbean* (Baltimore, 2014), 146–48, 172.

29. Fitzpatrick, *Writings*, 1:21.

30. See Wayne E. Stevens, Review of *Writings*, *MVHR* 20 (1933–34): 410–11.

31. See his obituary in the *New York Times* for 11 Dec. 1987. Jackson's publications include, for example, *Letters of the Lewis and Clark Expedition, with related documents, 1783–1854* (Urbana, Ill., 1962); *The Journals of Zebulon Montgomery Pike, with letters and related documents* (2 vols.; Norman, Okla., 1966); and *Thomas Jefferson & the Stony Mountains: Exploring the West from Monticello* (Urbana, Ill., 1981).

32. See her obituary in the *Daily Progress* (Charlottesville, Va.) for 8 Oct. 2011.

33. Donald Jackson to Frank E. Morse, 21 Sept. 1971 (Papers of George Washington Administrative Files, ViU).

34. *Journal of Southern History* 43 (1977): 432.

35. Kevin P. Kelly, Review of *Diaries*, *WMQ*, 3rd ser., 36 (1979): 627.

36. Robert Middlekauff, *Washington's Revolution: The Making of America's First Leader* (New York, 2015), 318, n.6.

37. See *DGW-Abridged* 8–15.
38. See, for instance, Chernow, *Washington*.
39. Sparks, *Writings*, 2:424.
40. Toner, *Daily Journal*, 7.
41. Fitzpatrick, *Diaries*, 1:16.

INTRODUCTION
COMING OF AGE AND A TRIP TO BARBADOS

History remembers George Washington as an iconic figure of noble character who commanded near-universal respect. Less considered are the painful personal losses and other obstacles that marked his path to success. The Barbados diary captures an ambitious young man on the cusp of adulthood, embracing a voyage that would prove to be a crucial turning point in his development.

Family and Boyhood

Augustine Washington (1694–1743), George Washington's father, occupied the second tier of Virginia gentry, influencing local matters but possessing little power in provincial affairs. As a Virginia planter, Augustine grew tobacco while also investing in ventures such as wool production and iron manufacturing.[1] As was then customary, he also acquired land and amassed property for his heirs.

American colonists prized English over local education, deeming it crucial for advancement to the highest ranks of colonial society. Accordingly, Augustine and his first wife, Jane Butler (1699–1729), sent their sons Lawrence (1718–1752) and Augustine Jr. (1720–1762) to Appleby School in England. Neither of the couple's two other children, Butler and Jane, survived to adulthood. In 1731, two years after his wife's death, Augustine Sr. married Mary Ball (c.1708–1789), who had inherited considerable property and possessions from her father and stepfather. Together, Augustine and Mary had six children. George, born in 1732 at Popes Creek plantation in Westmoreland County, was the eldest, and his siblings included Betty (1733–1797), Samuel (1734–1781), John Augustine (1736–1787), and Charles (1738–1799). Mildred, born in 1739, died in infancy. Following Augustine's death in 1743, Mary raised her five young children on her own while also managing the family farm. She remained a widow until her death in 1789.

George Washington was three years old when his father moved the family to Little Hunting Creek on the Potomac River—the future site of Mount Vernon; they moved again three years later to a plantation on the Rappahannock River that subsequent generations would name Ferry Farm. When young George was eight years old, the house was damaged by fire, about which David Humphreys queried Washington in his contemporary biography.[2] The widely accepted account that the fire had completely destroyed Ferry Farm was challenged by an archaeological investigation in 2008 that revealed a different story. Historical archaeologist Philip Levy and his colleagues discovered ample evidence that the fire was small and contained.[3]

Levy, author of *Where the Cherry Tree Grew: The Story of Ferry Farm, George Washington's Boyhood Home*, argues that Ferry Farm, a comfortable but modest house that served as Washington's primary residence until 1754, must be considered his seminal home. He traces the roots of Washington's character—of both living man and mythical figure—to his childhood residence. Mason Locke Weems's famous cherry tree account, had it been true, would have occurred when young George lived at Ferry Farm. And the Rappahannock was the river that the youth allegedly cleared with a stone, a myth that demonstrated his throwing ability in the same way as did the legend of his having thrown a silver dollar across the Potomac. At Ferry Farm, Washington experienced the birth and death of his infant sister Mildred, the fire just one year later, and the loss of his father three years after that. He was eleven years old and living at Ferry Farm when Mary became a single mother. She could not afford to send her son to England for schooling; instead, he was educated at Ferry Farm, where he learned about farming and discovered surveying, and this was the home he left behind when he accompanied his half brother Lawrence to Barbados.

Washington neither identified strongly with, nor compared himself to, his father.[4] Premature death was a common reality in eighteenth-century Virginia, and the loss of a parent could impact a child's life both emotionally and financially. When family stability was threatened or destroyed, children often relied on a network of friends and extended kin.[5] For Washington, this included his mother, half brothers Lawrence and Augustine Jr., and his father's family at Chotank in Stafford County, Virginia. In his last will and testament, he bequeathed his "gold headed Canes" and "Spy-glasses" to "the acquaintances and friends of my Juvenile years, Lawrence Washington & Robert Washington of Chotanck."[6] Even with the security of an extended family and the relative prosperity implicit in land ownership, young George endured loss and instability while seeking his place in the world.[7]

Career Influences of Lawrence Washington and the Fairfax Family

When his father died, Washington found himself without paternal guidance and bereft of formal education.[8] He also became a slaveholder and a landowner, inheriting ten slaves, Ferry Farm, and several other tracts through his father's will.[9] Lawrence, fourteen years his brother's senior, stepped in as patron to the young man. According to Dorothy Twohig, "Lawrence's virtual adoption of his younger half-brother was not unusual in colonial Virginia, where ties between brothers were frequently very close and where older brothers often assumed parental duties in matters of education and economic support."[10]

In George Washington's time, a patron and his dependent client maintained an unequal relationship. According to Fred Anderson, the latter's "was a status to be endured because the only path to becoming what he most wanted to be, a gentleman, ran through thickets of dependency that modern Americans would find bewildering, dense, and oppressive."[11] To advance in society, young men needed to learn the art of deference to their elders.

Lawrence was positioned well to extend the social connections and influence that his younger brother would otherwise have received from his father. After obtaining a

Lawrence Washington, oil painting by unknown artist, c.1743. (Courtesy of the Mount Vernon Ladies' Association)

formal English education, Lawrence embarked on a successful military career, serving as a captain in the Virginia Foot Regiments in the War of Jenkins' Ear, which began in 1739. He then joined the marines and served on Adm. Edward Vernon's Cartagena expedition as "the Senior Officer of those which were raised in [Virginia] & which with those of the other Colonies formed what was called the American Brigade."[12] Upon returning to his home colony, Lawrence became adjutant general of the Northern Virginia militia and was soon promoted to major. As Douglas Southall Freeman later concluded, "For the enlargement of George's mind and the polishing of his manners, Lawrence was almost an ideal elder brother."[13]

After he inherited Little Hunting Creek, Lawrence renamed the estate to honor Admiral Vernon, his erstwhile commander. Nearby was the Belvoir plantation, home of the powerful Fairfax family. In 1743 Lawrence enhanced his family's influence by marrying Ann Fairfax (c.1728–1761), the daughter of Col. William Fairfax (1691–1757) of Belvoir. William's cousin Thomas Fairfax (1693–1781), who had become sixth Lord Fairfax in 1710, controlled Virginia's Northern Neck, a considerable swath of land between the Rappahannock and Potomac rivers.[14] It is difficult to imagine a better patron for the fatherless young George Washington than Lawrence's father-in-law William Fairfax, who not only was wealthy and powerful in his own right but also was first cousin to arguably the most important landowner in Virginia at that time.[15] A letter that George wrote to his younger brother John Augustine on 28 May 1755 reveals his awareness of advantage; in it he advised the younger man to maintain a positive relationship with the Fairfaxes, because "it is in their power to be very serviceable upon many occasion's to us as young beginner's . . . for to that Family I am under many obligation<s> particularly to the old Gentleman [William Fairfax]."[16]

A young man so acutely aware of Virginia's hierarchical social structures might have found unsettling an earlier incident that was rife with class implications. In 1745, when George was thirteen years old, his brother Lawrence accused the Rev. Charles Green (c.1710–1765) of trying to "debauch Ann Fairfax now the wife of Major Washington whilst a maid,"[17] and the matter went to court. The suit likely posed a dilemma for Lawrence's young brother. Some years earlier, Augustine Washington Sr., as an elected vestryman of Truro Parish, had endorsed Green for rector.[18] Now Lawrence was bringing allegations that cast doubt on Green's character. According to historian Peter R. Henriques, the trial had more to do with power than with morality: "One essential reason for the trial was to assert planter hegemony and to punish a clergyman who challenged it." It was the "only full-scale ecclesiastical trial" in colonial Virginia.[19]

Green served as godfather for many Fairfax children, and the scandal shook his friendship with that family, to which young George was increasingly attached.[20] Although the thirteen-year-old may not have known the details of the trial, local gossip likely transmitted the more dramatic testimonies and arguments regarding sexuality, power, and influence—details interesting to a maturing young man. And though Green won the case after alleging that Ann Fairfax had been flirtatious, the verdict did not cause a breach between Washington and either of the parties involved. Perhaps as an early indication of his diplomatic talents, Washington kept cordial relations with the reverend until Green's death, and he certainly remained close with Lawrence and continued to strengthen his bonds with the Fairfaxes. The absence of a documentary record of his ruminations on this incident is lamentable, but the event is nevertheless important to the maturation of his character.

Sense of Adventure

The size of George Washington's library at the time of his death—some nine hundred books—reveals the importance he placed on reading. Various works related to travel and adventure feature his juvenile signature, suggesting the young man read or handled those volumes. Signed titles include Andrew Michael Ramsay's *The Travels of Cyrus . . .* (7th ed.; London, 1745) and Daniel Defoe's *A Tour Thro' the Whole Island of Great Britain . . .* (4 vols.; 4th ed.; London, 1748).[21] Like many young men, he sought out stories about exotic places and exciting adventures.

Perhaps to indulge this fascination with the unknown, Lawrence harbored aspirations of a life at sea for his younger brother. William Fairfax wrote to Lawrence in the fall of 1746 and alluded to the elder brother's desire to put fourteen-year-old George "to sea with good recommendations." Although Fairfax seems to have supported the plan, young George's mother opposed it.[22] Mary's half brother Joseph Ball suggested to her that in a life at sea, "they will . . . Cut him & Slash him and use him like a Negro, or rather, like a Dog."[23] Washington never revealed his opinion on the matter; he did, however, correct Humphreys's assumption that it was his father who had wanted to send him to the Royal Navy: "It was rather the wish of my eldest brother (on whom the several concerns of the family devolved)."[24] Nonetheless, his school exercise books for this period contain detailed notes and exercises in geography and mathematics, many of them drawn from navigational texts.[25]

Having set aside a prospective career at sea, Washington turned to surveying land, which, like the Royal Navy, presented real opportunities—rather than just literary ones—for exploration. From an early age, he demonstrated in his exercise books a familiarity with that occupation, which shared some approaches and techniques with maritime navigation. These school copy books include detailed descriptions of surveying, or "the Art of Measuring Land," in addition to sample land plats and math equations. Washington devoted pages to carefully illustrated exercises, including "How to lay out 100 Acres of Land in a Triangle whose Base and Perpendicular is equal" and a "Convenient Table shewing the length & breadth of an Acre,"[26] and soon sought opportunities to practice his new skills.

The respectable profession of surveying offered financial and social advancement, as well as the prospect of journeys into unknown wilderness, which must have appealed to the young reader of Defoe. Washington's first practical experience came by way of the Fairfax family in 1748. Lawrence's father-in-law, William Fairfax, acting as a land agent on behalf of Thomas Fairfax, invited young George to join his son George William Fairfax (1724–1787) on a surveying expedition to the Shenandoah Valley. This was Washington's first employment, and it occasioned his earliest known attempt to keep a daily record of his activities.

His journal from 11 March to 13 April 1748 is not a diary in the modern sense. In concise entries, the sixteen-year-old documented only what he believed to be important. He noted "beautiful Groves of Sugar Trees" and "thirty odd Indians" performing a "War Daunce." He also recorded complaints in greater detail than he would in subsequent diaries. Travel took him over "the Worst Road that ever was trod by Man or Beast." He encountered German settlers who "seem to be as Ignorant a Set of People as the Indians," and he endured an "Intolerably smoaky" evening.[27] Real adventure turned out to be less comfortable than the kind he found in books.

The entry for 15 March 1748 illustrates his inexperience. Upon settling into bed for the evening, Washington found to his "Surprize" that it was "nothing but a Little Straw." The lack of sheets proved less upsetting than the "one Thread Bear blanket with double its Weight of Vermin such as Lice Fleas &c." He waited until dark, rose from bed, "put on my Cloths & Lay as my Companions," and noted his lesson: "I made a Promise not to Sleep so from that time forward."[28]

Washington's first official appointment came in July 1749, when he was commissioned as a surveyor of Culpeper County, authorized to make public surveys in Virginia. For more than three years, he surveyed land in eastern Culpeper County and in less-settled Frederick County, receiving surveying assignments from the proprietary land office at Belvoir. The young man's family ties to the well-connected Fairfaxes likely helped him to secure preferred missions.[29] In a letter to Thomas Fairfax in the fall of 1749, Washington described a visit to Belvoir, noting that "as your Lordship was not at Home I was inform[ed] by Colo. G. Fairfax that you had not any Directions in Particular more than were given to the other Surveyors as your Lordship had mentioned" and "therefore have made bold to Proceed on General Directions from him."[30]

As a surveyor, Washington was well-positioned to acquire more land, and in 1750 he bought 453 acres in Frederick County. The grant from Thomas Fairfax confirmed "a certain Tract of waste and ungranted Land" to "Mr George Washington of the County of King George." He would purchase six more tracts in Frederick County before 1754.[31]

While George advanced his surveying career, Lawrence was beset by a threatening illness. On 5 May 1749, the younger Washington wrote to his older brother, "I hope your Cough is much mended since I saw you last, if so likewise hope you have given over the thoughts of leaving Virginia."[32] Lawrence had not abandoned these thoughts, and he traveled to England later that year for a brief visit before returning to Virginia.[33] The following year, Lawrence sought benefit from "Warm Springs" in the Virginia wilderness, an excursion George supported with a loan of 14s. 8d.[34]

Weighty concerns involving surveying commitments and his brother's health likely left Washington with little patience for foolishness. In summer 1751, Ann Carrol and Mary McDaniel, two "Serv[an]ts of Fredericksburgh," were jailed on suspicion of felony and charged with "robing the Cloaths of Mr George Washington" while he bathed in the Rappahannock River. Their sentence came down on 2 Dec., when Washington was in Barbados: Carrol was acquitted, but McDaniel suffered "fifteen lashes on her bare back."[35] Probably nothing more than a youthful stunt, the theft clearly offended him enough to press charges, most likely in part because it violated his sense of modesty.[36]

With the final disposition of the case pending, Washington recognized that his brother's health took priority. He agreed to accompany Lawrence on an excursion to Barbados, which offered hopes for a cure for Lawrence as well as a chance for adventure on the high seas and in the exotic West Indies. Washington's financial accounts indicate the brothers' whereabouts in the weeks leading up to the voyage. Assuming he collected the sum in person, young George was at Mount Vernon on 10 Aug. 1751, when his sister-in-law Ann paid cash to satisfy a small loan that he had extended to her husband the previous month. Also in August, he lent Lawrence £3 18s. for a trip to Annapolis. There is no evidence that George accompanied him there.[37] Financial accounts place the younger Washington in Fredericksburg on 20 Aug., when his brother-in-law Fielding Lewis (who had married George and Lawrence's sister Betty) advanced him £41 6s. 2d. in "Cash" and "Guinea's."[38] At Mount Vernon on 12 Sept., George William Fairfax paid him £11 16s. 3d. for miscellaneous debts.[39]

Lawrence's continued respiratory ailments dispelled any lingering doubts about going to Barbados.[40] His wife could not accompany him: Ann Fairfax Washington was busy caring for their infant daughter Sarah, born at Mount Vernon in 1750. Only twenty-three years old when her husband left for Barbados, Ann had lost three infant children between 1745 and 1749, and it was surely out of the question to expose little Sarah to the perils of travel.

George's presence meant his brother need not travel alone. Besides fulfilling filial duty, accompanying Lawrence on a sea journey to the West Indies must have piqued the curiosity of the adventurous young surveyor, and he undoubtedly anticipated social and professional benefits from new island experiences and acquaintances.

In Barbados

After an arduous sea voyage that lasted longer than a month, the Washingtons' ship nearly missed the island altogether. The sight of land must have been a welcome surprise. As contemporary traveler Robert Poole described his own approach to Barbados, "Its first Appearance from the Sea, to the Eastward, is somewhat hilly; to the South-

West and North-West, more level. Its Surface appears generally covered with a graceful Verdure, by the growing of Sugar-Canes, &c. and is so every where furnished with Inhabitants, that it much resembles a scattered Village in the Midst of a Garden."[41]

While the terrain must have been novel and fascinating to the provincial surveyor, he likely sensed nothing overly strange in the white colonists' culture or domestic interiors. With Virginians reliant on trade with England as well as with the mother country's other colonies and those of Europe, Washington already had been exposed to a variety of goods from other nations, most likely ranging from chinaware and French silk to Dutch linen and Madeira wine. English, French, Dutch, and Spanish colonies in the Americas and in the Caribbean islands participated in an economic system that included the African continent as well as Europe.[42]

Island of Barbados, oil painting by Isaac Sailmaker, c.1694, with Bridgetown and Carlisle Bay in center foreground. (Yale Center for British Art, Paul Mellon Collection)

The brothers landed on Barbados on 2 Nov. and found an island flush with sugarcane and populated by roughly three slaves for every white colonist.[43] Within the white population, the poor outnumbered the planter elite.[44] By contrast, the Washingtons had left behind a Virginia population that was roughly half slave and half free.[45]

Though he was a slaveholder since age eleven, George Washington likely had not witnessed the level of brutality he encountered on the island. John Benson of Rhode Island recorded his impressions of slavery on Barbados during a 1760s visit, describing "the heads of slaves, fixed upon sharp pointed stakes, while their unburied carcases were exposed to be torn by dogs and vultures on the sandy beach."[46] Sailor Edward Thompson expressed horror at the treatment of slaves in Barbados in 1756 in similar terms, observing that the "cruel tyranny exercised over the slaves, is shocking to humanity," and noting in detail the punishment for a slave girl's "trivial domestick error," as her mistress "commanded four of her servants to hold her down to the ground, while she absolutely exulted in smiles, and dropped hot sealing wax on the different parts of the back, till the poor creature expired in the most excruciating tortures."[47] If young Washington saw or heard about similar atrocities, he omitted comment in his diary.

Notwithstanding the disturbing aspects of island life, the tropical climate and medical expertise of its doctors offered Lawrence hope for relief from his illness. One of the foremost physicians on Barbados was William Hillary (1697–1763), a Quaker born in Yorkshire, England, who had earned his medical degree from the University of Leiden in the Netherlands in 1722. As a student of Herman Boerhaave, Hillary approached the practice of medicine using the scientific method, based upon observation and facts. He was among the first physicians in England to scientifically correlate weather with disease. Hillary's first book, *A Rational and Mechanical Essay on the Small-Pox. . . .* , was published in 1735, and a second edition followed in 1740.[48] On 4 Nov. 1751, the second complete day the brothers spent on the island, Washington wrote that Hillary, the "eminent physician recommended by Major Clarke," visited Lawrence "to pass his opinion on my brother's disorder, which he did in a favorable light, giving great assurances that it was not so fixed but that a cure might be effectually made."

Hillary's willingness to treat Lawrence indicates the reach of the Fairfax connection. Deborah Clarke Fairfax (c.1705–c.1747) was a direct link between the Washingtons and Barbados gentry. The stepmother of Lawrence's wife, Ann Fairfax Washington, she was also the sister of the elder Gedney Clarke. Born in Salem, Mass., Gedney Clarke Sr. (1711–1764) played an active and lucrative role in the web of economic connections among British Atlantic colonies. Through investments in plantations, and trade in commodities such as rum, sugar, and slaves, Clarke strengthened his economic ties to the North American mainland while establishing himself as one of the most powerful merchants on Barbados. He owned three thousand acres in the Northern Neck of Virginia, granted by Thomas Fairfax, as well as two homes on Barbados—one in Bridgetown and another in the countryside of St. Michael Parish called Belle (Bell) Plantation. Clarke also served as a member of the Barbados Council and as collector of customs for Bridgetown.[49] As soon as the Washingtons arrived on the island, Clarke invited them to dine with him and his family.

The younger Washington contracted smallpox during his island visit. The diary jumps from 16 Nov. to 12 Dec., when he wrote that he "Went to Town" to visit the Clarke family, who "visited me in my illness and contributed all they cou'd in sendg me the necessary's required in that disorder." Hillary's book on smallpox lists the treatments Washington may have endured: bleeding during the high initial fever; purging and bleeding during the second fever; and consumption of medicines, fluids, and a special diet to decrease inflammation.[50] Washington's recovery conferred immunity to the disease for the rest of his life.[51]

During the twenty-four days he was healthy, Washington found time for leisure on the island. He met many of the island elite, whose overtures demonstrated respect to both brothers. Among several invitations that the Washingtons received during a dinner of the Beefsteak and Tripe Club on 9 Nov., the most generous came from a "Mr Maynard," who "desir'd and even insisted as well as his Lady on our coming to spend some Weeks with him and promis'd nothing shoud be wanting." An invitation from a militia officer resulted in a meal "with some Ladys" on 12 Nov. at Charles Fort.

Emerging into manhood, Washington noticed the women on Barbados and perhaps was noticed in turn. In his 22 Dec. overview of the island and its culture, he wrote that "The Ladys Generally are very agreeable but by ill custom . . . affect the Negro Style." Competition between Barbadian and European men for wives resounds in the 30 Sept. 1732 *Barbados Gazette*, in which "Barbadian Batchelors" accused their countrywomen of "throwing yourselves away in Wedlock, captivated by strange Faces, fine

Dresses, and deceitful Hearts." The public plea continues: "We believe that no Island in the Universe, for its Bigness, can shew greater Numbers of fair and lovely Women, than does this little Spot of our Nativity."[52] Perhaps Washington's "strange face" and "fine dress" attracted the attention of the island ladies. For his part, though, notions of romance may have carried him homeward. The first known letter he sent after returning from Barbados was to resume a courtship he had begun before leaving Virginia.[53]

All known information indicates that during his leisure time in Barbados, Washington conducted himself with the decorum expected of a Virginia gentleman. Along with a visit to the theater and various dinners with Barbadian elites, the social norm included church attendance. On Sunday, 10 Nov., he "went to Evening Service," and on 15 Dec. he attended Christ Church.

In his record of his first surveying mission, Washington had divulged both positive impressions and annoyances. Three years later, he offered introspection and opinions more sparingly in his diary of the Barbados trip. For example, in his 14 Nov. description of the theatrical performance of *The London Merchant: or, the History of George Barnwell*, he noted only that "the charactar of Barnwell and several others was said to be well perform'd." He would develop a lifelong love of the theater, but his opinion on what presumably was his first experience of it sadly remains unknown.

The brothers journeyed to Barbados with high hopes for Lawrence's health. Given their standing and ambition, it is a reasonable assumption that they also anticipated social advancement. Lawrence did not recover, but young George appears to have fulfilled the other objective to a considerable degree.

Moving Forward Despite Disappointed Hopes

Because the climate of Barbados had failed to improve his health, Lawrence sought elusive relief in Bermuda while his younger brother returned to Virginia.[54] But Bermuda offered no cure, either. With his health steadily declining, Lawrence traveled home to say goodbye to his wife and infant daughter. He died at Mount Vernon in July 1752.

George endured a difficult voyage back to Virginia without Lawrence. He abandoned the meticulous measurements of the outgoing voyage, and his terse diary entries highlight difficulties. On 23 Dec., he wrote of waves that made "the Ship rowl much and me very sick." The heat of the sun on 26 Dec. was "troublesome"; 31 Dec. brought "violent winds"; and on 9 Jan., seasickness left him "a Criple." He noted "Squals of Rain, much, & very Large hail with violent Thunder" on 14 Jan., and he described the sea as "Mountainous" on several days.

Although Washington never again ventured beyond the North American mainland,[55] he harbored memories of the island and may have brought back souvenirs of fan and staghorn coral, which survive among the collections at Mount Vernon. He also maintained a belief in the healthfulness of tropical climates. On 25 April 1784, he wrote David Parry, governor of Barbados, to introduce his nephew Maj. George Augustine Washington, noting that "Bad health, & the advice of [the major's] Physicians induce him to try the Sea air," and hence the young man had embarked on a ship headed to Barbados. On the premise that it might become necessary for his nephew to seek amenable climates elsewhere, Washington wrote similar letters to the governors of several other West Indian islands.[56]

a

b

Souvenirs that Washington took home with him may have included two varieties of coral called sea fan (a) and staghorn (c). Also found off Barbados was a variety that Griffith Hughes called "palmed hart's-horn" (b), more widely known as sea ginger. (a and c, courtesy of the Mount Vernon Ladies' Association; b, from Griffith Hughes, ***The Natural History of Barbados*** [London, 1750], Special Collections, University of Virginia)

c

Young George Washington, wax model, 2006. Created in 2005 by a team of historians, scientists, and artisans, this life-sized wax figure depicts George Washington at nineteen, surveying the American wilderness. (Courtesy of the Mount Vernon Ladies' Association)

Washington cultivated ties with the Fairfax family throughout his life. He remained friends with George William Fairfax and George's wife, Sarah "Sally" Cary Fairfax (c.1730–1811), for whom he displayed a strong attachment. He cryptically shared his affections for Sally in a letter to her on 12 Sept. 1758, noting that "the World has no business to know the object of my Love." He then asked in a letter dated 25 Sept.: "Do we still misunderstand the true meaning of each others Letters?"[57] The last time he wrote to Sally, who by then had been living in England for twenty-five years, was less than two years before his death. On 16 May 1798, he recollected "those happy moments—the happiest of my life—which I have enjoyed in your company."[58]

After his Barbados voyage, Washington's next foray into journaling began in late fall 1753, during his expedition to the Ohio Valley under the direction of Virginia lieutenant governor Robert Dinwiddie.[59] By this point, the cautious detachment he had displayed in the Barbados diary was replaced by a firm and commanding tone. His deference to others' opinions of a play's quality gave way to confidence in his own evaluations, as when he assessed a location for its strategic military potential: "I spent some Time in viewing the Rivers, & the Land in the Fork, which I think extreamly well situated for a Fort." The future Revolutionary War general can be glimpsed in his recollection that "[a]s I found many Plots concerted to retard the Indians Business, & prevent their returning with me, I endeavour'd all in my Power to frustrate their Schemes, & hurry them on to execute their intended Design."[60] Dinwiddie had the journal published, and the young man's self-assurance surely flourished as it garnered international attention.

Exceeding Expectations

Commander in chief of the Continental Army, hero of the Revolutionary War, first president of the United States of America: George Washington is today an icon of the nation he helped to create. However, aside from myths of a felled cherry tree and a silver dollar thrown across a river, his little-documented early years have played no discernable role in popular conceptions of his place in American history and culture. As a youth, he struggled to improve himself and attain greater stature in society. A crucial step in this process was his journey as a nineteen-year-old to Barbados, his first and only venture beyond the British North American colonies. George Washington grew up as a Virginian, but Barbados helped to shape him into the man who, in turn, helped to shape history.

---

1. See Warren, "Childhood of Washington," 5787.

2. See Zagarri, *David Humphreys' "Life of General Washington,"* 59. A response by GW has not been found. See also Robert Douglas to GW, 25 May 1795 (*PGW-Presidential* 18:173–75).

3. See Levy, *George Washington Written Upon the Land*, 130.

4. Warren, "Childhood of Washington," 5793.

5. See Darrett B. Rutman and Anita H. Rutman, *A Place in Time: Middlesex County, Virginia, 1650–1750* (New York, 1984), 120, quoted in Warren, "Childhood of Washington," 5794.

6. *PGW-Retirement* 4:486.

7. For more on GW's childhood, see Warren, "Childhood of Washington"; Zagarri, *David Humphreys' "Life of General Washington"*; and Levy, *Ferry Farm*.

8. See Anderson, "Washington's Mentors," 22.

9. See *PGW-Colonial* 1:5. For more on GW's inheritance, see Levy, *Ferry Farm*, 53–58.

10. Dorothy Twohig, "The Making of George Washington," in *George Washington and the Virginia Backcountry*, ed. Warren R. Hofstra (Madison, Wis., 1998), 8.

11. Anderson, "Washington's Mentors," 22.

12. Zagarri, *David Humphreys' "Life of General Washington,"* 8.

13. Freeman, *Washington*, 1:76–77.

14. For more information on the Fairfaxes, see Neill, *The Fairfaxes of England and America*.

15. See Anderson, "Washington's Mentors," 23.

16. *PGW-Colonial* 1:289–92.

17. "The Memorial of Sundry of the Magistrates, Vestrymen, Merchants & others of the Inhabitants of Truro Parish in Fairfax County," Green Papers, in Henriques, "Lawrence Washington Versus Charles Green," 247–48.

18. See Moxham, *Early Colonial Churches*, 7–8.

19. Henriques, "Lawrence Washington Versus Charles Green," 233, 235.

20. See Moxham, *Early Colonial Churches*, 8, 12.

21. Griffin, *Catalogue of the Washington Collection*, 67, 170. For more on GW and reading, see Ferraro, "Washington's Mind," 547–48.

22. For extracts from William Fairfax to Lawrence Washington, 10 Sept. 1746, and, on the same subject, from Robert Jackson to Lawrence Washington, 18 Oct. 1746, see Sparks, *Writings*, 2:415–16.

23. Joseph Ball to Mary Ball Washington, 19 May 1747, quoted in Chase, "A Stake in the West," 162.

24. Zagarri, *David Humphreys' "Life of General Washington,"* 7.

25. These include Seller, *Practical Navigation*, and Atkinson, *Epitome of Navigation* (1736); see also the introductory essay to "Sailing to Barbados." For a description of GW's school copy books, see *PGW-Colonial* 1:1–4.

26. LC-Copy Book 1, 27, 30. LC-Copy Book 2, 89.

27. *DGW* 1:7, 13, 12, 18–19.

28. *DGW* 1:10.

29. See Chase, "A Stake in the West," 171–72.

30. *PGW-Colonial* 1:39.

31. *PGW-Colonial* 1:47–48.

32. *PGW-Colonial* 1:6.

33. See *PGW-Colonial* 1:37–39. Lawrence Washington visited England for medical advice and business concerns regarding the Ohio Company.

34. LC-Ledger A, folio 4, left.

35. *PGW-Colonial* 1:48–49.

36. For another analysis of this incident, see Freeman, *Washington*, 1:246–47.

37. LC-Ledger A, folio 4. For a claim that the brothers went to Maryland together, see Freeman, *Washington*, 1:247.

38. LC-Ledger A, folio 8, right.

39. LC-Ledger A, folio 1, right.

40. For more on the purported health benefits of Barbados, see p. 51 in the introductory essay to "On the Island."

41. Poole, *Beneficent Bee: or, Traveller's Companion*, 213.

42. Scholars have labeled this system the Triangular Trade, the most well-known example of which is the transatlantic slave trade.

43. See Molen, "Population and Social Patterns in Barbados," 289.

44. See Keagy, "Poor Whites of Barbados," 9–52.

45. See *Historical Statistics of the United States: Colonial Times to 1970, Bicentennial Edition* (2 parts, Washington, D.C., 1975), 2:1168.

46. Matthew Parker, *The Sugar Barons: Family, Corruption, Empire, and War in the West Indies* (New York, 2011), 267.

47. Edward Thompson, *Sailor's Letters. Written to his Select Friends in England, during his Voyages and Travels in Europe, Asia, Africa, and America. From the Years 1754 to 1759* (2 vols.; London, 1766), 22–23.

48. See C. C. Booth, "William Hillary—A Pupil of Boerhaave," *Medical History* 7 (1963): 297–316.

49. See S. D. Smith, "Gedney Clarke of Salem and Barbados: Transatlantic Super-Merchant," *New England Quarterly* 76 (2003): 506, 508–15. For the governmental structure of Barbados, see p. 54 in the introductory essay to "On the Island."

50. See Hillary, *Small-Pox*, 27–29.

51. For more on the lasting benefits of his ordeal with smallpox, see p. 58 in the introductory essay to "On the Island."

52. Arthur, *Caribbean Treasure*, 56–58.

53. For more on GW's romantic pursuits, see p. 107 in the introductory essay to "Back in Virginia."

54. For portions of Lawrence's letters from the islands after GW's departure, see Appendix C.

55. For greater detail on why GW never traveled abroad again, see p. 82 in the introductory essay to "The Return Voyage."

56. *PGW-Confederation* 1:306.

57. *PGW-Colonial* 6:11, 41.

58. *PGW-Retirement* 2:272.

59. For background on the venture, see *DGW* 1:118–29. For more information on GW and Dinwiddie, see p. 104 in the introductory essay to "Back in Virginia."

60. *DGW* 1:132, 150.

THE BARBADOS DIARY

1751–52

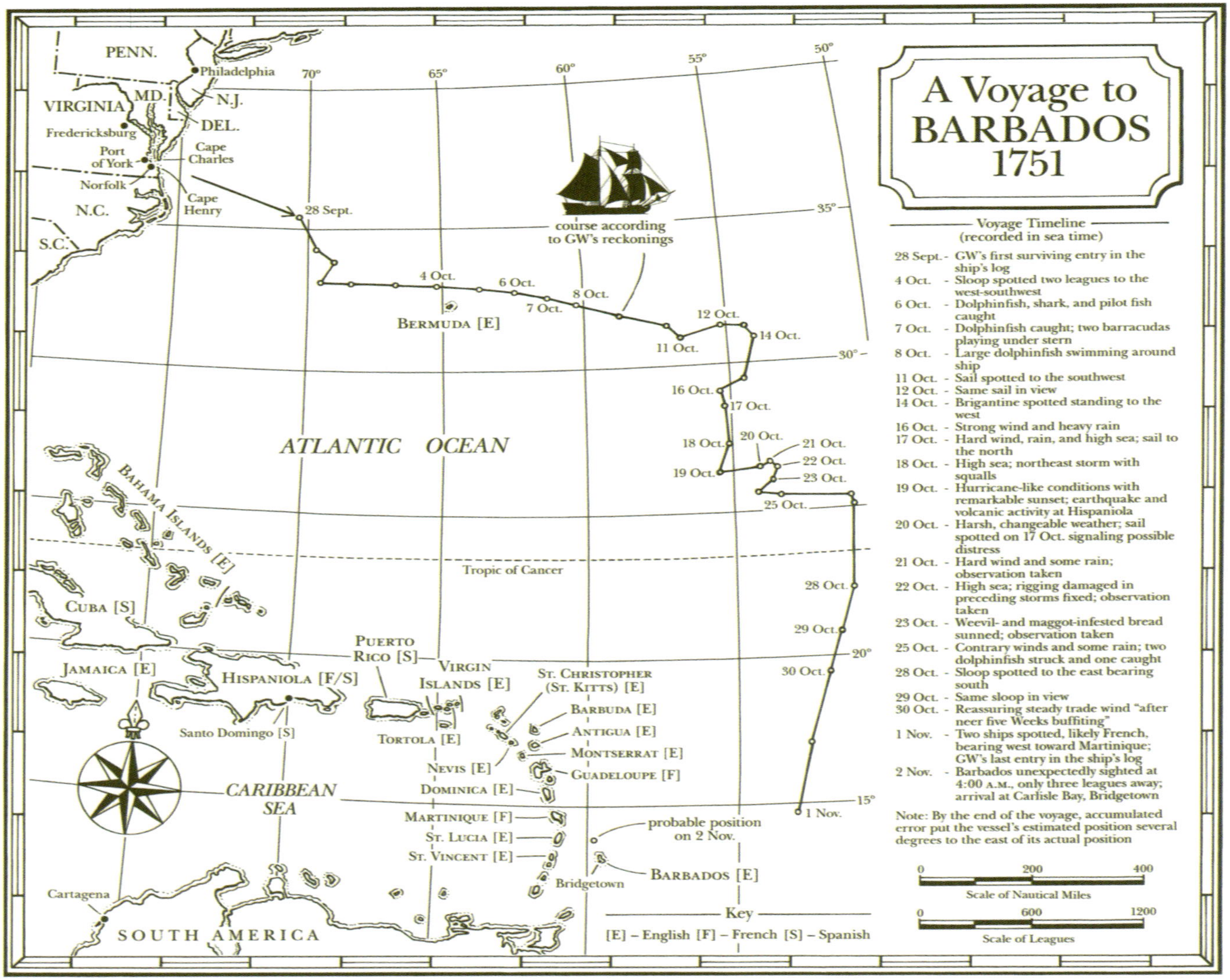

A voyage to Barbados, 1751. (Illustrated by Rick Britton. Copyright Rick Britton 2017.)

SAILING TO BARBADOS

C.25 SEPTEMBER–2 NOVEMBER 1751

The sea and sailing fascinated young George Washington and continued to interest him throughout his life. Books within his youthful reach and those he later acquired included volumes on rigging, seamanship, nautical math, and travel writing. His brother Lawrence's library featured Jonathan Swift's *Gulliver's Travels* (2 vols.; first published in 1726) and James Atkinson's *Epitome of the Art of Navigation* . . . , which appeared in several editions throughout the first half of the eighteenth century.[1] George owned the sixth edition of George Anson's *A Voyage Round the World* . . . (London, 1749), and he signed his copy of the English translation of Guillaume François Antoine de L'Hospital's mathematical text *An Analytick Treatise of Conick Sections* . . . (London, 1723) around March 1750. He also obtained Daniel Defoe's *Robinson Crusoe* (3 vols.; London, 1719–20); *A Voyage Round the World, In His Majesty's Ship The Dolphin, Commanded by the Honourable Commodore Byron* (London, 1767); and numerous other works.[2]

For his own purposes, Washington documented his voyage to Barbados in a ship's log, the traditional means of recording events and information to aid sea navigation. Printed books of blank charts available at the beginning of the eighteenth century show how common it was for mariners to keep logs.[3] Earlier editors and historians made little of his Barbados logbook. No diary extracts in Jared Sparks's *Writings* came from the out-

"A Ship describ'd," in James Atkinson, ***A Compleat System of Navigation*** . . . , Dublin, 1750. Atkinson introduced novice sailors to the parts of a ship: "I Shall here give you the Draught of a Ship, with her Rigging, that so you may not altogether be a Stranger to the Names of the Masts and Tackle at your first going aboard a Ship." (Courtesy of British Library)

bound journey. Without evidence, and certainly incorrectly, Sparks asserted that the data and calculations of Washington's first weeks at sea represented an "exact copy" of the captain's log. Although Sparks attributed remarks on weather conditions and events at sea to Washington, he deemed the land portion of the diary more interesting.[4] The next editor, Joseph Toner, treated the tables more seriously, claiming that Washington "took with regularity the daily, instrumental observations made by navigators at sea, doubtless under the immediate instructions of the captain." Toner presented the navigational information in his edition, but he did not analyze it closely.[5]

The Departure

The ship's log offers valuable insight into George Washington's youthful understanding of navigation, though much of what he may have recorded about the journey's beginning is missing. Lost and mutilated pages undoubtedly contained valuable information: the Washington brothers' vessel, port of departure, and date of sailing. Fragments believed to be from the initial account of the outbound voyage, summarized in the editorial note for 25–27 Sept., appear to have been written in standard paragraphs, not tables. Indeed, the brothers most likely were relegated to their quarters below deck those first days, when all hands would have been summoned to get the vessel out of the Chesapeake Bay and onto the open ocean.[6] By the time he definitely started dabbling in nautical calculations on 28 Sept., the ship was halfway to Bermuda.[7]

The ship on which the brothers sailed is not named in any surviving entry in the diary. Washington's scattered descriptions of it suggest a brigantine with two masts and both square- and fore-and-aft-rigged sails. The Virginia shipping lists for September 1751 specify no departures to Barbados at the middle or end of that month. The brig *Kingston* arrived at York (now Yorktown) from Barbados on 20 Sept., but a return voyage within a week is highly unlikely. The schooner *Fredericksburg*, which sailed on 2 or 3 Sept. from Port Rappahannock, is a possibility.[8] The best case can be made for the brigantine *Success*. Diary editors Donald Jackson and Dorothy Twohig claimed: "If the vessel did sail from the Potomac, it was the *Success*, [commanded by] Jeremiah Cranston, 40 tons, 8 men, carrying a cargo of 4,480 barrel staves, 7,627 feet of plank, 984 bushels of corn, and 31 barrels of herring."[9] Their examination of the shipping lists for the South Potomac customs office identified only one vessel sailing from there to Barbados within a time frame that put the brothers far at sea by 28 September. The records suggest a sailing date of 23 Aug. or 23 September. Jackson and Twohig concluded that, if the *Success* sailed in August, a delay after clearing port would not have been unusual before entering the river.[10]

Another examination of the South Potomac shipping lists yielded a previously unnoticed detail that lends more credence to the *Success* having carried the Washingtons to Barbados: John Dalton & Co. owned the vessel.[11] John Dalton (d. 1777) was a leading Alexandria merchant and had been in partnership since 1744 with John Carlyle (1720–1780), also of Alexandria. In 1747, Carlyle married Sarah Fairfax of Belvoir, the sister of Lawrence Washington's wife, Ann. George Washington later referred to Dalton as his "good Friend," and Dalton and Carlyle became his suppliers during the French and Indian War.[12] George and Lawrence likely heard of the *Success*'s impending voyage to Barbados through a Fairfax connection.

The *Success* was built in Hanover, Mass., in 1746 and was registered in Virginia at the South Potomac customs office on 30 Nov. 1749. The vessel made a trip to Barbados and returned to the Potomac in May 1751 with a cargo of rum, sugar, molasses, and sixteen slaves. Accounts from voyages between the island and Virginia in 1752 further identified the *Success* as a "brig" that occasionally carried passengers.[13] John Carlyle wrote his brother George in August 1752 that one of his ship's boys, or attendants, was "now In Barbados In our Brigantine Success."[14] The ship's owners—alternately listed as John Dalton & Co. or John Carlyle & Co.—finally sold "the Hull, which is laid up, and all the Materials of the Brigantine *Success*" at the end of November 1753.[15]

Sailing in the Mid-Eighteenth Century

The first half of the eighteenth century saw the growth of the maritime working class and the British shipping industry. At this time, merchant seamen began their careers in their late teens or early twenties and averaged twenty-seven years of age. A captain might be in his early thirties. Sailors traveled around the globe and often became quite worldly.[16]

The common sailor, or "tar"—identifiable by his wide-legged, ankle-high pants often weatherproofed with tar—had a distinctive gait suited to unsteady decks on tumbling seas. His speech was "unmistakable," a blend of "technical terms, unusual syntax, distinctive pronunciation, and a generous portion of swearing and cursing."[17] Washington adopted some technical terminology—the "handing" and "reefing" of sails, for instance—and imitated words he overheard, as in righting "the riggan" (see the entries for 5 and 22 Oct.). He certainly met men hardened by extreme weather conditions and the difficulties of life at sea. Sailors' skin was parched by the sun, beaten by the wind, and often variously tattooed, and untoward events or acts of violence resulted in mangled hands and bodies.

Sailors typically sought adventure and the promise of steady livelihoods. Many poor agricultural laborers took to the sea or sought employment in major port cities. Not a few sailors had been impressed into service or lured by wartime promises of high wages. The seaman's lot could be "likened to hell."[18] Newcomers serving in the West Indies faced higher mortality rates from disease than those found among their counterparts elsewhere in the world, along with the usual threats of shipwreck, hurricanes, and attack by privateers. Washington's experiences among sailors likely quelled his early aspirations to sea life.[19]

Daily Life: Work and Leisure

Washington most likely enlisted the supervision of the captain or a member of his crew, for a fee, to guide him through the processes of sailing and navigation as they unfolded daily. Such a shipboard apprenticeship was "a common practice in Europe during the seventeenth and eighteenth centuries, as attested in the works of Sir Jonas Moore, Samuel Pepys, and practical sea and math grammars of the period," according to maritime archaeologist and historian Jason Lunze. Young George would have had access to the captain's log as well as opportunities to test out the log-line, sandglass, octant, and various nautical charts.[20] His sometimes heavily edited text and his notations for "dead reckoning" and "observation" indicate that he took an active, if unofficial, role in noting corrected estimations of latitude based on direct observation of solar altitude when weather permitted (see the entries for 5, 16, and 20–23 Oct.). He also may have assisted with sails and rigging, often describing with the communal "we" the performance of these tasks.

Time on deck provided escape from the dark confinement and stifling air of quarters below. Fishing offered a welcome supplement to his diet, which, after a month at sea, would be compromised "by Weavel & Maggots" (see the entry for 23 Oct.). He encountered the dolphinfish, or mahi-mahi, and would have witnessed the fish change in color from bright blues and greens to a dull golden-gray when caught. He observed a shark and its accompanying pilot fish, as well as the unsuccessful attempt to catch another predator, the ferocious barracuda (see the entries for 6 and 7 Oct.).

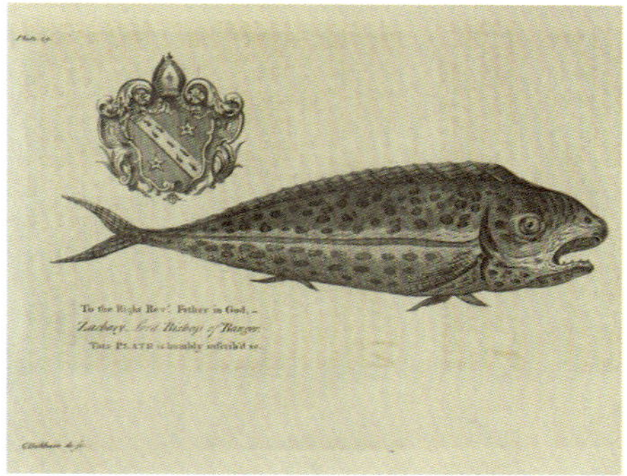

Dolphinfish (mahi-mahi), as depicted in Griffith Hughes, *The Natural History of Barbados*, London, 1750. (Special Collections, University of Virginia)

Surveyor of the Sea

Navigation captured Washington's interest during his five weeks at sea. The meticulous nature of his ship's log suggests something more than just a break from boredom. Clearly, his intellectual bent toward mathematics and experience as a practical surveyor suited him to the task. In addition, mapping the vessel's geographic coordinates likely offered the opportunity to socialize with the captain and crew. Keeping a logbook required precision, demonstrating his sense of responsibility and capacity for leadership.[21]

Washington probably learned how to keep "A Sea-Reckoning, or Journal," from James Atkinson's influential *Epitome of the Art of Navigation*, with its sample logbook for "an intended *Voyage* from the *Lizard* towards *Barbadoes*."[22] He already used a compass adeptly and could measure the terrain from three and a half years' experience as a surveyor. In an exercise book that likely dates to early 1748, he had rendered the 128 compass directions in Atkinson's "A Table of Angles."

Figuring out absolute position on open water posed greater challenges than doing so on land. Longitude could not be measured reliably at sea during the mid-eighteenth century. New techniques such as measuring lunar distances and keeping time on ship would not be perfected and in general use for decades.[23] While latitude could be determined by measuring the sun's altitude at noon (or that of other celestial bodies at night) and referring to a table of declinations, longitude had to be reckoned mathematically.

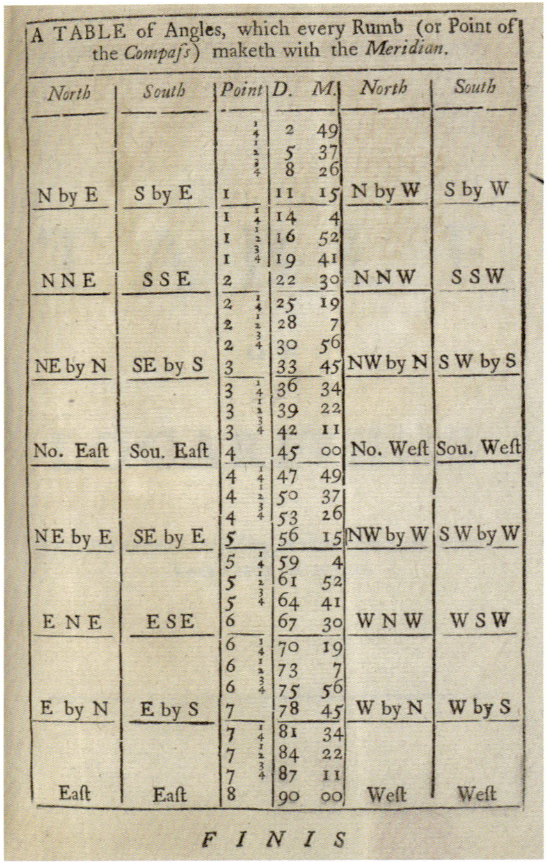

A TABLE of Angles, which every Rumb (or Point of the *Compaſs*) maketh with the *Meridian*.

North	*South*	*Point*		D.	M.	*North*	*South*
			1/4	2	49		
			1/2	5	37		
			3/4	8	26		
N by E	S by E	1		11	15	N by W	S by W
		1	1/4	14	4		
		1	1/2	16	52		
		1	3/4	19	41		
N N E	S S E	2		22	30	N N W	S S W
		2	1/4	25	19		
		2	1/2	28	7		
		2	3/4	30	56		
NE by N	SE by S	3		33	45	NW by N	S W by S
		3	1/4	36	34		
		3	1/2	39	22		
		3	3/4	42	11		
No. Eaſt	Sou. Eaſt	4		45	00	No. Weſt	Sou. Weſt
		4	1/4	47	49		
		4	1/2	50	37		
		4	3/4	53	26		
NE by E	SE by E	5		56	15	NW by W	S W by W
		5	1/4	59	4		
		5	1/2	61	52		
		5	3/4	64	41		
E N E	E S E	6		67	30	W N W	W S W
		6	1/4	70	19		
		6	1/2	73	7		
		6	3/4	75	56		
E by N	E by S	7		78	45	W by N	W by S
		7	1/4	81	34		
		7	1/2	84	22		
		7	3/4	87	11		
Eaſt	Eaſt	8		90	00	Weſt	Weſt

F I N I S

a

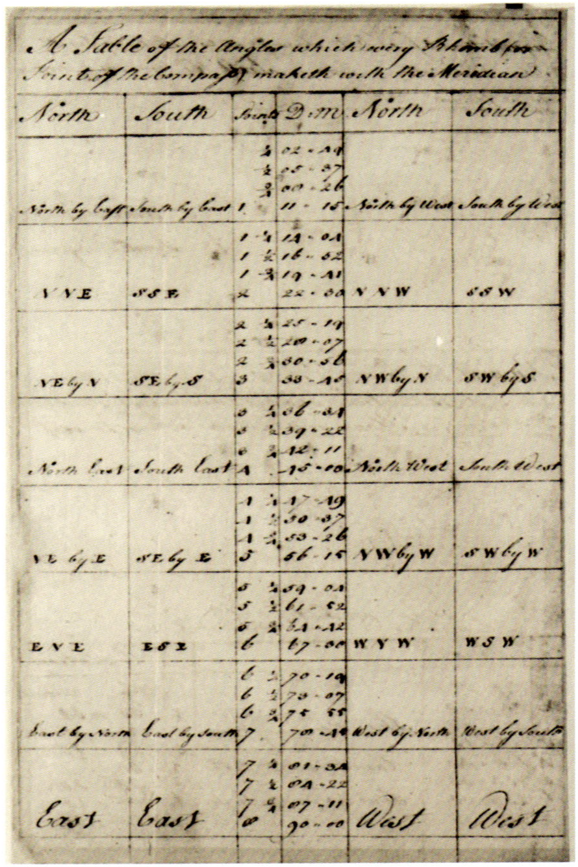

A Table of the Angles which every Rhumb or Point of the Compass maketh with the Meridian

North	South	Points	D. M.	North	South
North by East	South by East	1		North by West	South by West
N N E	S S E	2		N N W	S S W
N E by N	S E by S	3		N W by N	S W by S
North East	South East	4		North West	South West
N E by E	S E by E	5		N W by W	S W by W
E N E	E S E	6		W N W	W S W
East by North	East by South	7		West by North	West by South
East	East	8		West	West

b

Washington copied the "Table of Angles" (a) printed in James Atkinson's influential navigational texts from ***A Compleat System of Navigation . . .*** (Dublin, 1750) in his school exercise books (b). (a, courtesy of British Library; b, George Washington, Exercise Books 1745 to 1747: School Copy Book, Volume 2 in George Washington Papers, Series 1, Exercise Books, Diaries, and Surveys 1745–99, Subseries 1A, Manuscript Division, Library of Congress)

Although Washington presumably had read about the process in Atkinson's *Epitome of Navigation*, putting it into practice was another matter. For a detailed discussion of the procedures, see the "Comprehensive Chart of Navigational Data and Computations" (Appendix B).

Despite careful attempts to map the vessel's progress, its arrival at Barbados in the early morning hours of Saturday, 2 Nov., came as a revelation: "We were grea<tly a>larm'd with the cry of Land at 4 A:M: we quitted our Beds with Sur~~rp~~prise and found the <I>sland plainly appearing at <a>bout 3 leauges distance." According to "our reckonings," the vessel should have been 450 nautical miles to the east of the island (see the entry for 2 Nov., n.2). The common sailing technique was to reach the proper latitude while well to the east of the destination, and then "run down a westing."[24] If the vessel had missed Barbados and also St. Vincent, 94 nautical miles to the west, the Caribbean Sea loomed vast until Nicaragua another 1,300 nautical miles away. Washington's relief at avoiding this fate almost certainly offset the shock of the unexpected sighting.

Interpreting the Ship's Log

The ship's log is recorded in sea time as opposed to land, or civil, time. Each entry is a half day ahead of land time, running from noon on the previous day through noon on the present day. This time differential must be kept in mind to properly interpret the thirty-five tables that Washington recorded on his voyage. In the following example of a page from the ship's log, note that the left-hand column, indicating time of day, begins with 2:00 P.M. and ends with noon. The latter marked the start of a new day, according to sea time, and was the time of day when data along the bottom of the log was recorded. See also Appendix B for further details.

SHIP'S LOG

Hour	Knots (Speed)	Course	Winds	Remarks for [Date]
2 PM				
4				
6				
8				
10				
12 AM				
2				
4				
6				
8				
10				
12 PM				

Departure (naut. miles/day)	Course (average)	Distance (nm/day)	Difference of Latitude (°/′)	Latitude (°/′)	Meridian Distance (Total Departure) (nm)	Difference of Longitude (°/′)	Longitude (°/′)

A glossary of nautical terms used throughout the ship's log (as well as in the later record of the return voyage) can be found in Appendix A. For wind intensity, a chart of relative scales of terms follows. The information comes from Daniel Defoe and the more contemporary Thomas Thistlewood, with the later Beaufort Scale providing additional context.[25]

A CENTURY OF WIND FORCE SCALES

Scale #	Defoe, 1704	Thistlewood, 1750–86 (estimated average knots)	Beaufort, 1805 (knots)
0	Stark calm	Calm (0)	Calm (0)
1	Calm weather	Light airs and calms (3)	Light air (1–3)
2	Little wind	Light airs (3)	Light breeze (4–6)
3	A fine breeze	Light wind (8)	Gentle breeze (7–10)
4	A small gale	Moderate breeze (13)	Moderate breeze (11–16)
5	A fresh gale	Fresh breeze (18)	Fresh breeze (17–21)
6	A top-sail gale	Fresh gales (23)	Strong breeze (22–27)
7	Blows fresh	Strong gales (28)	Moderate gale (28–33)
8	A hard gale of wind	Hard (heavy) gales	Fresh gale (34–40)
9	A fret of wind	Storm	Strong gale (41–47)
10	A storm	Hurricane	Whole gale (48–55)
11	A tempest		Storm (56–63)
12			Hurricane (over 63)

Many of the tables are incomplete due to mutilations in the manuscript. Washington also omitted headings for many columns. Using as an example his entry for 7 Oct., the editors have supplied complete titles for both mutilated and blank columns. For a compilation of all geographic data, both recorded by Washington and editorially supplied, see Appendix B.

---

1. For these titles, see "An Inventory of the Estate of Lawrence Washington Esqr. deceased, as Apprais'd by us the Subscribers the 7th & 8th of March 1753" (ViMtvL).

2. GW's later acquisitions included Moore, *The New Practical Navigator* (1793); Steel, *The Elements and Practice of Rigging and Seamanship* (1794); Truxtun, *Remarks, Instructions, and Examples relating to the Latitude & Longitude* (1794); Walker, *A Treatise on Magnetism* (1794); and Guthrie, *A New System of Modern Geography* (1794–95). See *PGW-Colonial* 6:285, 287; 7:344–45; and Griffin, *Catalogue of the Washington Collection*, 13, 200, 217–18, 489, 505, 507, 546–47. Mount Vernon acquired the L'Hospital volume in 1999.

3. See, for instance, *A Logg-Book For the Use of Mariners. To which is Added, Proper Columns For the better Working A Travers at Sea* (London, 1710). For insightful commentary on keeping logbooks and their importance, see Gilje, *To Swear Like a Sailor*, 65–105.

4. Sparks, *Writings*, 2:424.

5. Toner, *Daily Journal*, 6–7, 21–38.

6. Editors' conversation with maritime archaeologist and historian Jason Lunze, spring 2016.

7. Earlier editors and biographers inaccurately claimed that GW left port on this date. See Sparks, *Writings*, 2:422; Toner, *Daily Journal*, 5–6; Fitzpatrick, *Diaries*, 1:16; Freeman, *Washington*, 1:248.

8. See P.R.O.: C.O. 5/1444, folios 42, 118 (verso), Naval Office Shipping Lists for Virginia. See also the diary entry for 5 Nov., n.2.

9. DGW 1:26.

10. See P.R.O.: C.O. 5/1445, folio 59, Naval Office Shipping Lists for Virginia, and DGW 1:26.

11. See P.R.O.: C.O. 5/1445, folio 59, Naval Office Shipping Lists for Virginia.

12. *PGW-Colonial* 1:63, 229, 274.

13. P.R.O.: C.O. 5/1445, folios 58, 63; 1446, folio 54, Naval Office Shipping Lists for Virginia.

14. John Carlyle to George Carlyle, 4 Aug. 1752, in John F. Carlyle, ed., *The Personal and Family Correspondence of Col. John Carlyle of Alexandria, Virginia* (privately printed, 2011; photocopy held by The Washington Papers, ViU).

15. *Maryland Gazette* (Annapolis) for 20 Dec. 1753.

16. For information on the eighteenth-century sailor, see Marcus Rediker, *Between the Devil and the Deep Blue Sea: Merchant Seamen, Pirates, and the Anglo-American Maritime World, 1700–1750* (Cambridge, England, 1987), 2–14.

17. Ibid., 11.

18. Ibid., 13.

19. For more on young GW's desire to go to sea, see p. xxxv in the introduction to this volume.

20. Editors' conversation with Jason Lunze, spring 2016.

21. See Atkinson, *Epitome of Navigation* (1736), 265–66, and the discussion in Gilje, *To Swear Like a Sailor*, 68.

22. Atkinson, *Epitome of Navigation* (1736), 265, 271.

23. See Dava Sobel, *Longitude: The True Story of a Lone Genius Who Solved the Greatest Scientific Problem of His Time* (New York, 1995).

24. For use of this navigational terminology, see Anson, *Voyage*, 148, and *Sailing Directions for the East-India or Oriental Pilot*, 5, 24, 29, 36, 55, 70.

25. See [Defoe], *Storm*, 21–22, and Chenoweth, "18th Century Climate of Jamaica," 22–40.

THE DIARY ENTRIES

◆

Fragmentary entries for 25–27 Sept. 1751, George Washington, Diary, 1751–52. (George Washington Papers, Series 1, Exercise Books, Diaries, and Surveys 1745–99, Subseries 1B, Manuscript Division, Library of Congress; photograph by Alicia K. Anderson and Lynn A. Price)

Wednesday, 25 September–Friday, 27 September 1751

Editorial Note. The earliest truly identifiable diary entry is a remnant that indicates "Saterday 28th." Preceding this are narrowly vertical fragments of what appear to be the inner margins of two facing manuscript pages. On these fragments, snippets of visible lettering suggest the text of three prior diary entries, but no more than five letters can be seen on any line of text. Legible letters suggest or form words such as "<ve>ssel," "sic<k>," "Gulf," and "<con>trary" (perhaps as in contrary winds), which certainly indicate a sea voyage.[1] Horizontal line breaks on one of the fragments may denote the beginning of entries for separate days. Capital "T" after the first break, and "F" after the second, logically begin the words "Thursday" and "Friday" for 26 and 27 Sept., respectively. Text above the first break probably belonged to an entry for Wednesday, 25 September.

1. For a literal transcription of these manuscript pieces that demonstrates their incoherence, see Toner, *Daily Journal*, 21.

Saturday, 28 September 1751

<Hour>	knts	Cour[se]s	Winds	Remarks for Saterday 28th[1]
	< >	EsE	NE	this 2<4 hours > of < >.

1. With sea time beginning at noon on the previous day, the surviving top portion of this entry shows information for the afternoon of Friday, 27 September. GW likely recorded his remarks at noon on Saturday, the end of that sea day.

Sunday, 29 September 1751

[Hour]	[Knots]	[Course]	[Winds]	[Remarks]
		< >S	EBN	Winds < >.

<Departure>[1]	Course	dist[anc]e	Diff[erenc]e of Lat[itud]e	Lat<itude>	<Meridian Distance>	<Difference of Longitude>	<Longitude>
	SEBS	89	M[inutes]:S[econds] 74	34°.29′	M[iles] 219 East	60′ East	69:55

1. For an estimate of the day's departure, see Appendix B. The first entry to preserve a complete row of GW's headings is that for 7 October.

Monday, 30 September 1751

<Hour>	Kts	Course	Winds	Remarks for ~~S~~Munday 30th
	4	SEBS	EBN	The ~~foregoin~~<g > at East < >.
		< >E	East	

Tuesday, 1 October 1751

[Hour]	[Knots]	[Course]	[Winds]	[Remarks]				
			<S>E[1]	Sail < > to the < >.				
<Departure>		Course	dist[anc]e	diff[erenc]e of Lat[itud]e	Latitude	<Meridian Distance>	<Difference of Longitude>	<Longitude>
<23> Wt		SW¾W	m[iles] 36[2]	28′ So.	33°.34′		28′	69.19

1. The first letter of this direction is supplied in Toner, *Daily Journal*, 22.
2. GW inadvertently wrote “Et” after the distance.

Wednesday, 2 October 1751

<Hour>	Kts	Course	Winds	Remarks for Wednesd<ay 2>d
	< >	up[1] <N>Et[2] < >	SSE ESE EBS	Got under < > Stay Sa<il > great< >.

1. This word is rendered as "n" in Toner, *Daily Journal*, 23.
2. For the first letter of this direction, see Toner, *Daily Journal*, 23.

Thursday, 3 October 1751

[Hour]	[Knots]	[Course]	[Winds]	[Remarks]
				Gib < > Mod< >.[1]

<Departure>	[Course]	[Distance]	[Difference of Latitude]	<Latitude>	<Meridian Distance>	<Difference of Longitude>	<Longitude>
m[iles] <11>9 Et	East	m[iles] 119	00°.00'	33°.37'	m[iles] 402 E<t>	142 Et	66<.14>

1. GW likely is referring to the jib sail and moderate winds.

Friday, 4 October 1751

<Hour>	[Knots]	[Course]	[Winds]	Remark's for Fryday 4th[1]
<2>	3½	East	North	This Twenty four hours clear Weather & Little Wind with great Sea from the No. Ward.
4	4			
6	3½		NBE	
8	2½			
10	1½			
12	1½			D[itt]o Weather & Clear.
2	1½			
4	1½			
6	2			
8	2		NWt	discover'd a Sail bearing WSW distance 2 Leagues She appears to be a sloop standg to the Et W[ard].
10	2½			
<1>2	3	East	WNW	

[Departure]	[Course]	[Distance]	[Difference of Latitude]	[Latitude]	[Meridian Distance]	[Difference of Longitude]	[Longitude]
<58> Et	East	58	00.00	33.37	460	00°.70' Et	65.<04>

1. This is the first largely complete daily entry in the ship's log that survives. Jared Sparks, who initialed his comment, noted on this page of the manuscript: "I suppose this to be a fragment of a journal at Sea by Gen. Washington dur[ing] his voyage to ~~Bermuda~~ Barbadoes with his brother. . . . Oct. 1751."

Saturday, 5 October 1751

<Hour>	[Knots]	[Course]	[Winds]	Remarks for Saturday ~~6~~5th
<2>	3½	East	No.Wt[1]	Theis ~~Last~~ 24 hours had ~~but Little~~ Moderate[2] Winds from the No. with Smooth Sea & clear weather made all the Sail we cou'd—~~put to~~ righted all ~~our~~the riggan.
<4>	3			
5[3]				
6	3½		~~NB~~Et	
8	~~2~~3½		No.	
10	~~1~~3½			
12	~~1~~2½	East	No.	
2	~~1~~3½			
4	~~1~~3½			
6	~~2~~3½			
8	~~2~~3½		~~NWt~~	
<1>0	2½			
<12>	~~3~~2	East	~~WNo.W~~No.	

[Departure]	[Course]	[Distance]	[Difference of Latitude]	[Latitude]	[Meridian Distance]	[Difference of Longitude]	[Longitude]
<7>3 Et	EBS	75	00.13 S	33°.24'	533 Et	87 Et	63.37

1. GW inserted "Wt" over dashes.
2. GW's change to this word presumably reflects his edits to knots in the column for ship speed.
3. GW typically noted only even-numbered hours.

Sunday, 6 October 1751

<Hour>	Kts	Course	Wind	Remarks for Sunday ~~7~~6th[1]
<2>	3½	East	North	Th~~e~~is ~~preceding~~ Day for the first part little Winds Fair Weather & smooth Sea.
<4>	3			
6	2½			
8	2½			Catched a Dolphin at 8 P.M. a Shark at 11 & a ~~p~~One of his pilot fish the Dalp[h]in & pilot fish was dressed for Dinner.[2]
10	2½			
12		} Calm		
2				
4				
6	1			Sprung up a Little breeze of Wind at WSW which Waver'd to & from the No.
8	1½			
10	1½			
<12>	1½	East	West	

[Departure]	[Course]	[Distance]	[Difference of Latitude]	[Latitude]	[Meridian Distance]	[Difference of Longitude]	[Longitude]
m[iles] 39 Et	E½S	m[iles] 39 D[ay]	00°.3' No.[3]	33°.27'	m[iles] 572 Et	00:46' E	62°.<51'>

1. GW penned the numeral over an ellipsis, suggesting that he added the date later. For similar renderings, see the entries for 10 and 20 October.

2. There are two species of dolphinfish: the mahi-mahi and its more diminutive cousin, the pompano. Pilot fish often accompany sharks. Both the dolphinfish and pilot fish are good for eating, the former having "very excellent meat, being dress'd by a good hand" (Ligon, *True & Exact History*, 4).

3. Either GW mistook the direction, according to the average course, which indicates southward movement, or the latitude was corrected through direct observation at noon. See the entries for 12 Oct., n.1, and 21 Oct., n.2.

Monday, 7 October 1751

Hrs	Kts	Course	Winds	Remark's for Munday 7th
<2>	1½	East	SW	But Little Wind at SWt & So. with calm smooth Sea and fair Weather Saw many fish swimming abt us of which a Dalphin we catchd at Noon but cou'd not intice with a bait-ed hook t~~o~~wo Baricoota's which played under our Stern for some Hours[1] the Dalp[h]in being small we had it dressed for Supper.
4	1½			
6	1½			
8	1½	ESE		
10	1½			
12	3		South	
2	2			
4	1½			
6	1½			
8	1½			
10	2½			
<1>2	2½	ESE	South	

<D>ep[ar]t[ur]e	Course	dist[anc]e	Diff[erence] Lat[itud]e	Latitude	M[eridia]n dist[anc]e	Diff[erenc]e Long[itud]e	Longitude
<4>6 Et	E¼S	m[iles] 46 D[ay]	00°.2' So.	33°.25'	M[iles] 618 Et	00°.55' Et	61°.54'[2]

1. A ferocious predator, the barracuda can reach up to seven feet in length.
2. This calculation introduces a small error in the longitude (see Appendix B).

TUESDAY, 8 OCTOBER 1751

<H>R	KTS	COURSE	WINDS	REMARKS FOR TUESDAY 8TH
<2>	3½	ESE	SW	Small Wind at SW with Smooth Sea & fair Weathr was attended by a large Dalp[h]in swimg around the ship that wou'd not be insnar'd by any bait w~~oeud~~cou'd lay.
<4>	2½			
6	2			
8	1½			
10	1½			
12	2	ESE	SW	
2	3½			
4	4			
6	3½		WSW	
8	3½			
10	4			
<1>2	4	ESE		

<D>ep[artur]e M[iles]	[Course]	[Distance]	[Difference of Latitude]	[Latitude]	[Meridian Distance]	[Difference of Longitude]	[Longitude]
m[iles] 66 E	ESE	71 D[ay]	00°.27' S	32°.58'	684 E	01°.19' E	60<.35>

Wednesday, 9 October 1751

<Hr>	Kts	Courses	Winds	Remarks for Wednesday 9th
<2>	3	ESE	WSW	Fine clear Weather with moderate Gale<s> of Wind and smooth Sea for the first part the latter was favour'd with a brisker Wind.
<4>	2½			
6	2½			
8	3½		SW	
10	4			
12	4½			
2	4½			
4	4½			
6	5		SW	
8	5			
<1>0	5½		WSW	
<12>	5½	ESE		

<D>ep[ar]t[ur]e	Course	dist[anc]e	diff[erenc]e of Lat[itude]	Latitude	M[eridia]n dist[anc]e	Diff[erenc]e Long[itude]	Longitude
<9>4 Et	EBS¾S	100 D[ay]	00°.31' S	32°.27'	778 Et	01°.50' Et	58°.45'

Thursday, 10 October 1751

<H>r	Kts	Courses	Wind	Remarks for Thursday 10th[1]
<2>	5½	SE	WSW	
<4>	6			
<6>	5½			
8	5			Clear Weather Moderate Breese & Smoo<th> Sea.
10	4½			
12	4½	SE	WSW	
2	4½			
4	5			
6	3½		WNW	
8	3			
<1>0	3			
<12>	2½	SE		

[Departure]	[Course]	[Distance]	[Difference of Latitude]	[Latitude]	[Meridian Distance]	[Difference of Longitude]	[Longitude]
86 E	SEBE	105 D[ay]	00°.57'	31°.30'	864 E	01°.40' E	57.<05>

1. GW penned the numeral over an ellipsis, suggesting that he added the date later. For similar renderings, see the entries for 6 and 20 October.

Friday, 11 October 1751

Hr	Kts	Courses	Wind	Remarks for Fryday 11th
<2>	2½	SSE	WNW	Light Breese of Wind for the first part which died away Espyed a Sail at 3 PM. to the SWt.
<4>	2			
6	1½			
8	1			
10	1			
12				
2		Calm		
4		Calm		
6		Calm		
8		Calm		
10				
<1>2	2½	EB[N][1]	SEBE	

<D>ep[ar]t[ur]e E	[Course]	[Distance]	[Difference of Latitude]	[Latitude]	[Meridian Distance]	[Difference of Longitude]	[Longitude]
<5> M[iles]	SBE	27 D[ay]	00°.26' S	31°.04'	m[iles] 870 E	00°.6' E	56.59

1. GW inadvertently wrote "EBW" for this direction (see the first notation under "Courses" for 12 Oct.).

Saturday, 12 October 1751

<H>r	Kts	Courses	Wind	Remarks for Saturday 12th
<2>	3½	EBN	SEBS	~~Fr~~<e>~~sh~~h<a>rd gales of Wind at SSE and wavering with clear & pleasant Weather—saw the sale mention'd the preceding day.
<4>	3			
<6>	3	East	SSEt	
8	3½			
10	3½			
12	3½			
2	5			
4	3			handed the Sprit Sail & flying Jib.
6	3			
8	3½			
<1>0	3			
<1>2	3			

[Departure]	[Course]	[Distance]	[Difference of Latitude]	[Latitude]	[Meridian Distance]	[Difference of Longitude]	[Longitude]
79 M[iles]	EBS	81	00°.14' N[1]	31°.18'	m[iles] 949 Et	01°.32' Et	5<5°.27'>

1. Either GW incorrectly recorded north, as the day's average course indicates southward movement, or the latitude was corrected through direct observation. See the entries for 6 Oct., n.3, and 21 Oct., n.2.

Sunday, 13 October 1751

Hr	Kts	Course	Wind	Remarks for Sunday the 13th of O.
<2>	3[1]	EBS	SBE	Light and variable Winds have attend<ed> this Day with hazey Weather & some Squals of small rain: R[eefed]F[foretop]S[ail] at 10 PM.
<4>	3			
6	2	EBS½S	South	
8	3			
10	2			
<1>2	2	ESE	South	
2	3			
4	3			
6	3	EBS	SBEt	
8	2	~~S~~[E]SE	So.	
<1>0	2	SSE	SW	
<1>2	1½			

[Departure]	[Course]	[Distance]	[Difference of Latitude]	[Latitude]	[Meridian Distance]	[Difference of Longitude]	[Longitude]
<5>9 M[iles]	East	m[iles] 59 D[ay]	00.00	31°.18'	m[iles] 1008 Et	01°.09' E	54.18

1. A horizontal line with marks above and below follow this numeral, suggesting that GW considered recording a fraction.

Monday, 14 October 1751

<Hour>	[Knots]	[Course]	[Winds]	Remarks for Munday 14th
<2>	2	ESE	South	Light & variable Winds for the 1st part the Latter Calm with a great Swell from the Southward Saw a Sail at 2 pM at 4— discover'd her to be a Brigantine standg to the Westward.
<4>	2			
6	1½	SBEt	SWBW	
8				
10				
12		Calm[1]		
2				
4				
6				
8				
<1>0	3	Sh	Et	
<1>2	2½			

[Departure]	[Course]	[Distance]	[Difference of Latitude]	[Latitude]	[Meridian Distance]	[Difference of Longitude]	[Longitude]
<18> Et	SEBE	m[iles] 22 D[ay]	00°.12' S	31°.06'	1026	00°.21' Et	<53°.57'>

1. Written in unusually large script, this word runs across the columns for course and winds.

Tuesday, 15 October 1751

<Hour>	Kts	Course	Wind	Remarks for Tuesday 15th
<2>	3	So.	EBS	Fresh and Wavering Gales with < > contending Seas from Southwar<d> & No. Ward.
<4>	4			
<6>	4			
8	4			
10	4		ESE	
12	3½	SSWt	SEt	
2	3			
4	3			
6	3	SWBS	SEBS	
8	2½			
10	3	SSW	SE	
<1>2	3	SWBS	SEBS	

[Departure]	[Course]	[Distance]	[Difference of Latitude]	[Latitude]	[Meridian Distance]	[Difference of Longitude]	[Longitude]
19 W	SBW	m[iles] 80 D[ay]	01°.16' S	29°.50'	m[iles] 1007 Et	00°.22' W	54°.19'

Wednesday, 16 October 1751

<H>r	Kts	Course	Wind	Remarks for Wednesday 16th
<2>	4	SWBS	[S]EBS[1]	The first part fresh & wavering Winds with some Squals of Rain the Latter Strong Wind with hard Squals which turnd to a heavy settled Rain at 8 PM. [Handed] M[ain]T[op]S[ail] at AM 6 R[eefed]**F**[foretop]S[ail] at 10 D[ouble]R[eefed] **F**[foretop]S[ail] at 11 [Handed]**F**[foretop]S[ail].[2]
<4>	3½			
<6>	3½	SW	SSE	
8	3½	SWB~~S~~W	SBE	
10	3			
12	3½			
2	3	WSW	So.	
4	3½			
6	4½			
8	4			
<1>0	3½			
<1>2	2			

[Departure]	[Course]	[Distance]	[Difference of Latitude]	[Latitude]	[Meridian Distance]	[Difference of Longitude]	[Longitude]
<75> W	WSW	80	M DR[3] S 30	d R 29[°].20'	932 Et	01°.26'	55.<45>

1. This wind direction follows the last one GW noted for 15 Oct., rather than the inadvertent "EEBS" he rendered on the manuscript.
2. The progressive taking in of sail responds to the increasingly stormy weather.
3. "DR" in this and the latitude column stand for dead reckoning (see the entry for 20 Oct.).

Thursday, 17 October 1751

<Hour>	Kts	Course	Wind	Remarks for Thursday 17th
<2>	2	ESE	SBW	Hard gales of Wind and rain 'till 4 PM: wh<en> the Wind got to the Westward and moderated a<t> 12 was calm with a disturb'd and large Sea which eminently endanger'd our masts roling a way[1] 'till releiv'd by a small No. Wt breese at 2 A:M ~~from the No. Wt~~ we crouded all the Sail we cou'd to steady her going which scarcely had the desir'd effect ~~at: 10~~Discover'd a Sail standing to the No. Ward of us at 10 A:M.
<4>	1½			
6	1½	SBE	WSW	
8	1			
10	1		NWt	
12			Calm	
2	1		NW	
4	1			
6	1½			
8	1½			
<1>0	2			
<12>	2½	SBE	No.	

[Departure]	[Course]	[Distance]	[Difference of Latitude]	[Latitude]	[Meridian Distance]	[Difference of Longitude]	[Longitude]
25 Et	SE½Et	33 D[ay]	00°.21'	28°.59'	957 Et	00.29' Et	55°.16'

1. The vibrations of a "rolling" ship in an agitated sea can result in masts being damaged, loosened, or lost.

Friday, 18 October 1751

<H>r	Kts	Course	Wind	Remarks for Friday 18th
<2>	3½	SBE	No.	A Large Sea & Some Squals of Rain ~~&c~~: fresh Breeze 'till 2 AM ~~when~~ the wind died away & rem[aine]d calm untill 9 with Settled Rain~~s~~ when ~~the~~a NEt Storm & Squals of Rain Suceeded the rain with intermission the wind withou<t>.
<4>	5			
6	4½		NEt	
8	4½			
10	5			
12	5			
2	4½			
4		}		
6			Calm	
8				
<1>0	6½	SBE	NEt	
<12>	7½			

[Departure]	[Course]	[Distance]	[Difference of Latitude]	[Latitude]	[Meridian Distance]	[Difference of Longitude]	[Longitude]
<9> Et	S½Et	92 D[ay]	01°.31' S	27°.28'	966 Et	00°.10' Et	<55°.06'>

Saturday, 19 October 1751

<Hour>	Kts	Course	Wind	Remarks for Saturday 19th
<2>	4			Hard Squals of Wind and rain with a f<er>mented[1] Sea ~~running no way~~ jostling in heaps[2] occasion<ed> by the Wavering wind which ~~for the who~~<~~le~~> in <this> 24 hours ~~has~~ Veer'd the Compass ~~&~~ not remain~~d~~ing 2 hours in any point the Seamen seem'd disheartned confessing they never had seen such weather before it was universally ~~allow'd~~ surmis'd their had been a violent hurricane not far distant a prodigy in the West appear'd towards the suns setting abt 6 [P]M[3] remarkable for its extraordinary redness.[4]
<4>			Calm	
6	2	SWt	No.Et	
8		Try up	No. of NNW	
10				
12	~~1~~3	South	East	
2	3			
4	2½			
6			Calm	
8			D[itt]o	
<1>0	1	SW	SEt	
<1>2	1			

[Departure]	[Course]	[Distance]	[Difference of Latitude]	[Latitude]	[Meridian Distance]	[Difference of Longitude]	[Longitude]
<1>2 Wt	SSW	m[iles] 33 D[ay]	00°.30' S	26°.58'	m[iles] 954 Et	00°.14' W	55.20

1. An alternative reading might be "fomented," but the editors judge the missing particle of manuscript to be wider than one might expect to accommodate a single letter.

2. A 1737 treatise used "jostling in heaps" to describe chaos: "[O]nce there was nothing but Atoms, jostling in Heaps, and crouding one upon another, and not the least Understanding or Design to govern them" ("An Enquiry in the Law of Nature and Revelation. To which is annexed, A Discourse concerning the Mediator between God and Men," London, 1737, 6).

The previous struck-out phrase, "running no way," echoes Daniel Defoe's ***Robinson Crusoe***: "[B]eing between the two great Currents, . . . in the wake of the Island, I found the Water at least still and running no Way" (166). The popular novel saw four editions in its first year of publication, and GW likely knew the work. He later acquired a three-volume set of *Robinson Crusoe* from the Custis estate (see *PGW-Colonial* 6:283–84, 287; 7:343–45), and he owned Defoe's next favorite, *Tour thro' Great Britain*, whose title pages all bear GW's early signature (see Griffin, *Catalogue of the Washington Collection*, 67).

3. GW inadvertently wrote "AM" for the time.

4. A geologic rather than meteorologic event, over 800 nautical miles to the southwest of GW's vessel, caused the unusual sea and sun. At about 2:00 P.M. on 18 Oct., an earthquake shook Hispaniola and "a Volcano opened within 20 leagues of *Domingo*, ejecting fire and smoke" (*Gentleman's Magazine* for February 1752, p. 91). A "prodigy" is a remarkable occurrence often considered foreboding.

SUNDAY, 20 OCTOBER 1751

<HOUR>	KTS	COURSE	WIND	REMARKS FOR SUNDAY 20TH[1]
<2>	4[2]	SBEt	NEt	~~C~~A Constant succession of hard Winds, Squals of Rain, & Calms was the remarkable attendants of this day which was so sudden & flighty we durst not go under any but reefd Sails & those that we coud D[ouble]R[eef] at 6 AM put abt to the Eastward ~~at~~A Sloop that for the two preceding Days was <in> sight of us[3] hung out a Signal but wheth<er in> distress or not we are uncertain if it had <we> were incapable of releiving them by the contr[adictio]n of <winds>.[4]
<4>			Calm	
<6>	2	SW	N~~W~~Et	
8		Try up	No. of NNW	
10		~~So.~~	Et	
12	3	So.	Et	
2	3			
4	2½			
6			Calm	
8				
<1>0	1	SW	SEt	
<1>2	1			

[Departure]	[Course]	[Distance]	[Difference of Latitude]	[Latitude]	[Meridian Distance]	[Difference of Longitude]	[Longitude]
<3>7 E	EBN¾N	40 D[ay]	DR 00°.13' N	dr 27°.11'	991	00°.4~~1~~2' Et	54<.38>

1. GW penned the numeral over an ellipsis, suggesting that he added the date later. For similar renderings, see the entries for 6 and 10 October.

2. GW copied the data in this and the next three columns for speed, course, and winds from the entry for 19 October. His "Remarks" and the bottom row of computations, however, are unique to this entry.

3. GW first noted the vessel in his entry for 17 October.

4. Any attempt to assist the sloop positioned to the north would have required the difficult maneuver of sailing into prevailing winds blowing from the northeast.

Monday, 21 October 1751

<Hour>	Kts	Course	Wind	Remarks for Munday 21st
<2>	2½	ESE	So.	This Day was not much inferiour to th<e> foregoing only the Wind was not quite so <waver>ing tho' hard with some Squals of Rain <that> oblig'd us to lay too at 8 [P]M. at 6 [A]M.[1] ma<de> Sail with the wind at SW. and moderate undr R[eefed]M[ain]F[ore]S[ail] & D[ouble]R[eefed]**F**[foretop]S[ail].
<4>	3	EBS	SBE	
<6>	2½			
8		Try up	ESE of Et	
10				
12				
2				
4		up SE of	EsE	
6				
8	2	SEBS	SW	
<10>	2½			
<12>	2			

[Departure]	[Course]	[Distance]	[Difference of Latitude]	[Latitude]	[Meridian Distance]	[Difference of Longitude]	[Longitude]
<29> Et	NEBE	35 D[ay]	00°.19'	ob.[2] 27°.30'	1010	00°.33' Et	54.05

1. Likely in error, GW wrote "AM." for the first time and "PM." for the second.

2. This latitude was found through observation rather than calculation (see the entries for 22 and 23 Oct. for similar notations). Hadley's octant was the instrument then in vogue for taking the required astronomical measurements (see John Hadley, "The Description of a new Instrument for taking Angles," 147–57).

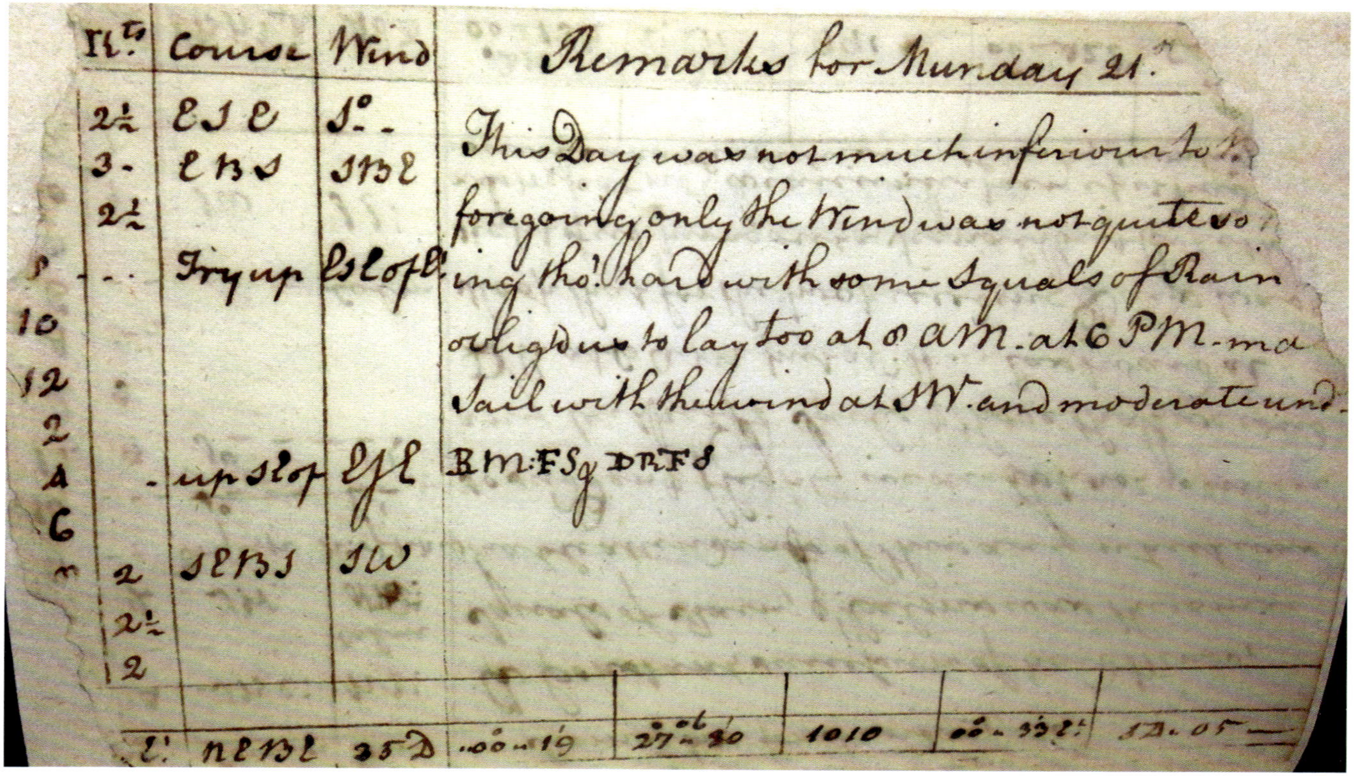

Remarks for Munday 21st

This Day was not much inferiour to the foregoing only the Wind was not quite so[...]ing tho' hard with some Squals of Rain obligd us to lay too at 8 AM. at 6 PM. ma[de] Sail with the wind at SW. and moderate und[er]

Entry for 21 Oct. 1751, George Washington, Diary, 1751–52. (George Washington Papers, Series 1, Exercise Books, Diaries, and Surveys 1745–99, Subseries 1B, Manuscript Division, Library of Congress; photograph by Alicia K. Anderson and Lynn A. Price)

Tuesday, 22 October 1751

<Hour>	Kts	Courses	Winds	Remarks for T~~H~~uesday 22d
<2>	1½	SSEt	SWt	Light ~~Bree~~ & Wavering Winds with a large tumbling Sea running many ways by the Various winds we have lately had all hands we busily employ'd in refitting the Riggan which had suffer'd much in the preceding Storms.
<4>	2			
<6>	2½			
<8>	1½	SBEt	SWBWt	
10	1½	South	WSW	
12	2			
2	1			
4	1½			
6	1			
8			Calm	
<10>				
<12>				

[Departure]	[Course]	[Distance]	[Difference of Latitude]	[Latitude]	[Meridian Distance]	[Difference of Longitude]	[Longitude]
8 Et	SSEt	21 D[ay]	00°.19' So.	Ob. 27°.11'	1018 Et	00°.09' Et	5<3°.56'>

Wednesday, 23 October 1751

<Hour>	Kts	Course	Wind	Remarks for Wednesday 23d
<2>		}	Calm	Calm 'till 8 [P]M[1] with a considerable Sw<ell> the wind freshen'd up at East with fine ~~Weather~~& regaling Weather[2] Sun'd our Bre<ad> which was almost Eaten up by Weavel & Maggots.[3]
4				
6				
8				
10	2	So.	Et	
12	1½			
2	2	SBWt	SEBE	
4	2			
6	3	SSW	SEt	
8	3			
10	3			
<12>	2½	SWBW	SBE	

[Departure]	[Course]	[Distance]	[Difference of Latitude]	[Latitude]	[Meridian Distance]	[Difference of Longitude]	[Longitude]
<1>2 Wt	SSW	32 D[ay]	Ob. 00°.29' S	26°.42'	1006 Et	00°.14' [W][4]	54°.10'

1. GW inadvertently wrote "AM" for the time.
2. "Regaling" here means pleasant and refreshing.
3. A naturalist wrote in 1750 that the grain weevil was "so commonly found in decayed Corn and Flour in every Part of the World, that it scarce deserves a particular Description" (G. Hughes, *Natural History of Barbados*, 87).
4. GW inadvertently wrote "Et" for the difference of longitude.

THURSDAY, 24 OCTOBER 1751

<HOUR>	KTS	COURSE	WIND	REMARKS FOR THURSDAY 2[4TH][1]
<2>	2½	SWBW	SBE	Fresh Breeses of Wind at SSE & wavering to the So. ward with pleas'ant Weathr & Smooth Sea at 8 A:M made a tack to the Eastward.
<4>	3	SWBS	SEB~~E~~S	
<6>	3			
8	2½	SW	SSE	
10	4			
12	4			
2	3	SWBW	SBE	
4	2			
6	2½	SW	SSE	
8	2½	SWBW	SBE	
<1>0	3	ESE	So.	
<1>2	2½			

[Departure]	[Course]	[Distance]	[Difference of Latitude]	[Latitude]	[Meridian Distance]	[Difference of Longitude]	[Longitude]
<35> W	SW½W	46 D[ay]	00°.29'	26.13	971 Et	00.39' [W][2]	<54°.49'>

1. GW erroneously wrote "22d" for the date.
2. As on the preceding day, GW inadvertently wrote "Et" for the difference of longitude.

Friday, 25 October 1751

<Hour>	Kts	Course	Wind	Remarks for Fryday 25t<h>
<2>	2½	ESE	So.	Moderate but contrary Winds from <the> SSWt to SSEt at 9 P:M: Struck two < > Dalphins one of wch was lost at < > grew hazey and thick: with some Squals of Rain from So. Et: Dalphin dress'd for Dinner.
<4>	2			
6	2	EBS	SBEt	
8	2			
10	2			
12	3			
2	3	ESE	So.	
4	4			
6	4	SEBE	SBW	
8	2½			
10	3	EsE	So.	
<1>2	2½	SEBEt	SBW	

[Departure]	[Course]	[Distance]	[Difference of Latitude]	[Latitude]	[Meridian Distance]	[Difference of Longitude]	[Longitude]
54 Et	E¾S	55 D[a]y	00 08'	26°.05'	1025 Et	01°.00'	53.49

Saturday, 26 October 1751

<Hour>	Kts	Course	Wind	Remarks for Saturday 26th
<2>	3	SE	SSW	Hazey with contrary Winds & smooth Sea.
<4>	2			
<6>	3			
8	3			
<10>	3			
12	3½			
2	3			
4	2½	SEBS	SWBS	
6	3½			
8	3½			
<1>0	3½	SSE	SW	
<12>	< >			

<Departure>	[Course]	[Distance]	[Difference of Latitude]	[Latitude]	[Meridian Distance]	[Difference of Longitude]	<Longitude>
<69 E>	ESE	75 D[ay]	00.29' S	25°.36'	<1094> Et	<01>°<.>16' Et	<51°.05'>[1]

1. GW probably calculated this incorrect estimate (see Appendix B for the correct longitude).

SUNDAY, 27 OCTOBER 1751

<HOUR>	<KNOTS>	<CO>URSE	WIND	REMARKS FOR <SU>NDAY 27<TH>
<2>	< >	< >S~~W~~E	SW	Light Winds & wavering from S<W> till 8 p:M: when it shifted to No. W. <and> died away with Rains succeeding ~~Rai~~<~~ns~~>.
<4>	< >	SBE	SWBW	
6	3[1]	So.	NW	
8	3			
10				
12		}	Calm	
2				
4	2	South	North	
6	1½	West	SSW	
8			Calm	
<1>0			D[itt]o	
<1>2	1	So.	No.	

[Departure]	[Course]	[Distance]	[Difference of Latitude]	[Latitude]	[Meridian Distance]	[Difference of Longitude]	[Longitude]
<0>	So.	28 D[ay]	00°.28' S	25.08	1094 Et	00.00	51°.05'

1. Marks after this numeral suggest that GW considered recording a fraction.

Monday, 28 October 1751

<Hour>	Kts	Course	Wind	Remarks for Munday 28th
<2>	7½	South	ENEt	Fresh gale of Wind at ENE came on at noon[1] with hazey Weather & some rain; it shifted to the Eastward and moderated: at 6 A:M saw a Sail to the Eastward bearing our course, made her to be a Sloop: Unbent mended and set ~~our~~the Main topsail
<4>	7½			
<6>	8½			
<8>	8½			
<10>	8½		East	
12	8			
2	5½			
4	3½			
6	1½	SBWt	SEBEt	
8	1½	South	EsE	
10	2½	SSW	SE	
<12>	< >	SWBW	SBE	

<Departure>	[Course]	[Distance]	[Difference of Latitude]	[Latitude]	[Meridian Distance]	[Difference of Longitude]	<Longitude>
<6 W>	<S>½W	132 D[ay]	02°.12'	22°.5<6>'	<1088> Et	<00°.07' W>	<51°.12'>

1. GW is referring to the end of the previous sea day.

Tuesday, 29 October 1751

<Hour>	<Knots>	<C>ourse	Wind<s>	Remarks for <T>uesday 2<9th>
<2>	< >	<S>SWt	SE	Wavering but pleasant gales of <Wind> with Fair open weather: the af<oresaid> Sloop still kept to windward bear<ing> her former course.[1]
<4>	< >	SBW	SEBE	
<6>	2½	South	EsE	
8	4½		EBS	
10	4½			
12	4½			
2	5	SBW	SEBE	
4	5	South	SBE	
6	5½			
8	5½		East	
<1>0	5½			
<1>2	5½			

[Departure]	[Course]	[Distance]	[Difference of Latitude]	[Latitude]	[Meridian Distance]	[Difference of Longitude]	[Longitude]
5 Wt	S¼W	103	01°.43'	21°.13'	1083 Et	00°.06' W	51°.18'

1. The sloop headed south by west (see the entry for 28 Oct.).

Wednesday, 30 October 1751

<Hour>	Kts	Course	Wind	Remarks for Wednesda<y 30th>
<2>	5	SBW	East	This Morning ~~was~~ agreeably ~~awa<k'd>~~ ~~with~~ arose with assurances of a certain & steady trade Wind which after neer five Weeks buffiting & being toss'd by a fickle & Merciless Ocean was gladening knews: the preceeding night we seperated from <the> sloop ab[ov]e mentioned.[1]
<4>	5			
<6>	5			
8	4½			
10	6½			
12	6½			
2	5			
4	5			
6	5			
8	4½			
<10>	4½			
<12>	< >		ENEt	

<Departure>	[Course]	[Distance]	[Difference of Latitude]	[Latitude]	[Meridian Distance]	[Difference of Longitude]	<Longitude>
<23 W>	SBW	128 D	1.57 S	19°.16'	<1060> Et	<00°.>24' <W>	<51°.42'>

1. For the sloop bearing the same course as GW's vessel, see the entries for 28 and 29 October.

Thursday, 31 October 1751

<Hour>	<Knots>	<Co>urses	Winds	Remarks f<or Thursda>y 3<1st>
<2>	< >	SBW	ENE	Regaling and G~~ale~~entle Gales f<rom the> Eastward, with hazey weather, & < > rain~~s~~: the latter part clear & pleas<ant> Weather.
<4>	< >			
<6>	4½			
<8>	5½			
10	5½			
12	5½	SBW		
2	5½		East	
4	5½		EBS	
6	5½			
8	6½			
<10>	5½			
<12>	5½	SBW		

[Departure]	[Course]	[Distance]	[Difference of Latitude]	[Latitude]	[Meridian Distance]	[Difference of Longitude]	<Longitude>
<13> W	SBW	130 D[ay]	2°.7' S	17°.09'	1047 Et	00°<.14'>	<51°.56'>

Friday, 1 November 1751

<Hour>	[Knots]	[Course]	[Winds]	Remarks for Friday the <1st>
<2>	6	SBW	East	Fine pleasant bree~~z~~ses with Fair Weather & smooth Sea. at 11 A:M Espy'd two Ships bearing West which we conjectur'd to be Frenchmen bound for Martineca they being in the Latitude thereof.[1]
<4>	6			
<6>	6			
8	6			
10	6			
12	6	SBW	East	
2	5½			
4	5½			
6	5½			
<8>	5½			
<10>	5½			
<12>	< >	SBW	ENEt	

<Departure>	[Course]	[Distance]	[Difference of Latitude]	[Latitude]	[Meridian Distance]	[Difference of Longitude]	<Longitude>
<27>	<SB>W	13<9>[2]	2°.16' S	14°5<3>'	<1020> Et	<28'>	<52°24'>

1. Then a French colony, Martinique is situated at 14°39' north latitude. Although GW's estimated longitude suggests that his vessel was over 500 nautical miles to the east of the island, the ship actually was much closer (see the entry for 2 Nov. and p. 9 in the introductory essay to "Sailing to Barbados").

2. Here GW recorded the difference of latitude, which appears to be the same as that in the adjacent space, but wrote the distance over it in darker ink.

Saturday, 2 November 1751

<Saturday 2d>[1]

We were grea<tly a>larm'd with the cry of Land at 4 A:M: we quitted our Beds with Sur~~rp~~prise and found the <I>sland plainly appearing at <a>bout 3 leauges distance wh<en> by our reckonings we shou'd have been near 150 Leauges to the Windward we to Leew<a>rd <a>bt the distance above mentiond[2] and had we been but 3 or 4 leauges more we shoud ~~not~~ have ~~s~~been <o>ut of sight of the Island run down the Latitu<de a>nd probably not have discover<ed the> Error in time to have gaind <the Is>land for 3 Weeks one Mon<th.>

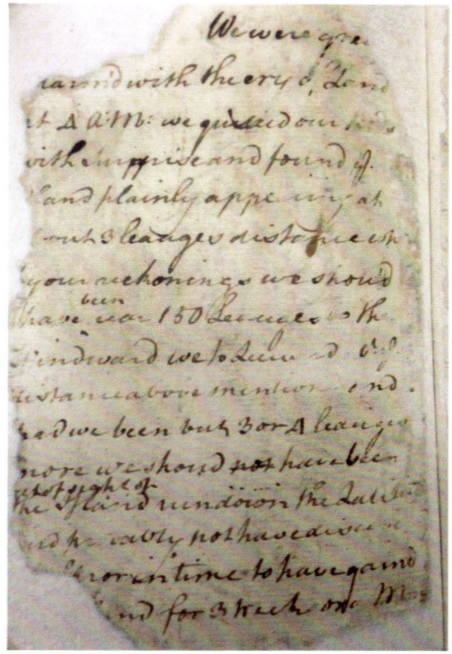

Entry for 2 Nov. 1751, George Washington, Diary, 1751–52. (George Washington Papers, Series 1, Exercise Books, Diaries, and Surveys 1745–99, Subseries 1B, Manuscript Division, Library of Congress; photograph by Alicia K. Anderson and Lynn A. Price)

1. The mutilated top left corner of this page probably included the dateline. GW now resumed land (or civil) time. He oriented the pages vertically and wrote in standard paragraph format from this entry to the conclusion of the diary.

2. GW's estimate placed the vessel 150 leagues, or 450 nautical miles, to the east of Barbados. In actuality, the ship stood some 10 nautical miles west of the island. The error in calculations accrued incrementally over the course of the voyage.

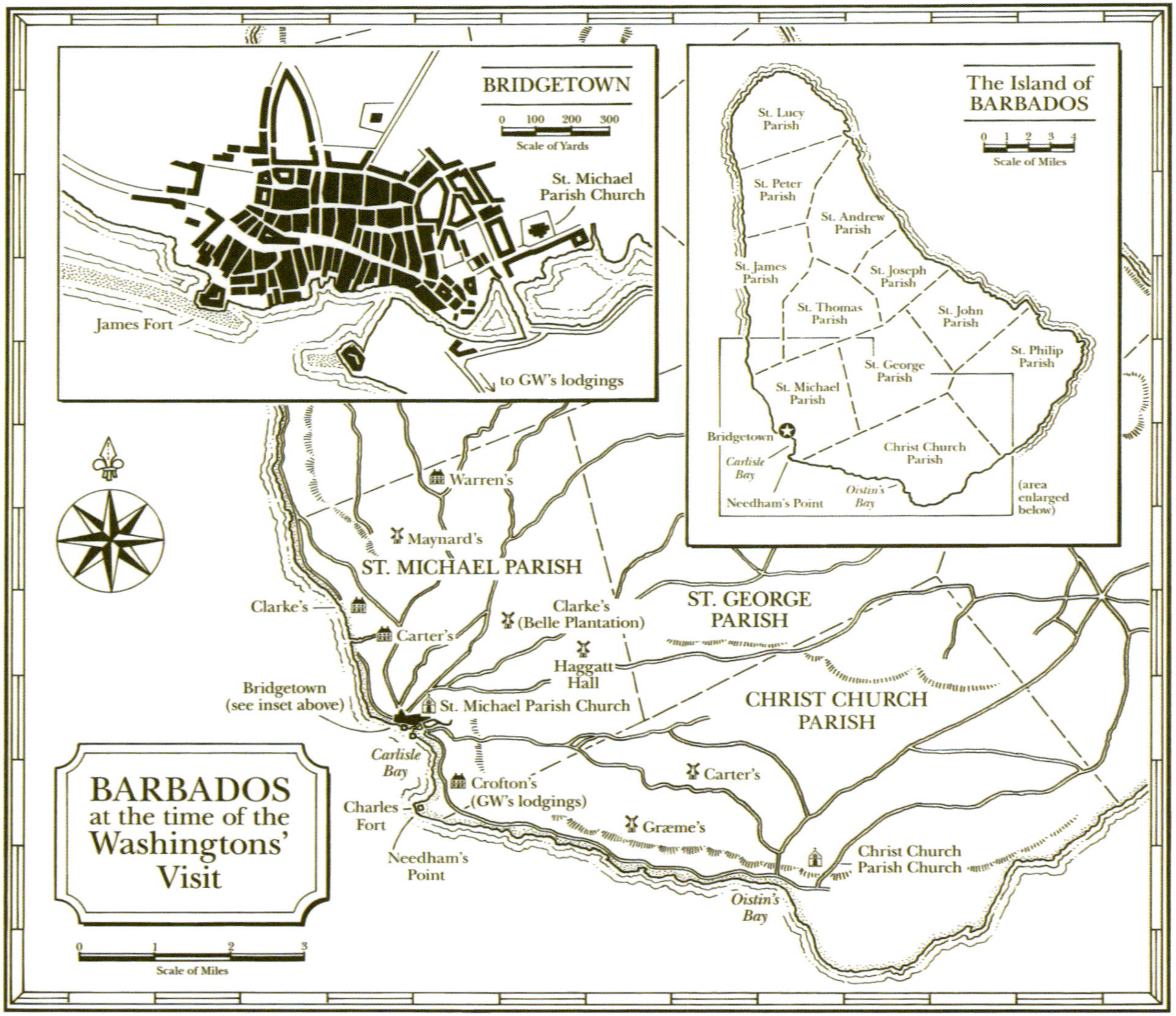

Barbados at the time of the Washingtons' visit. (Illustrated by Rick Britton. Copyright Rick Britton 2017.)

ON THE ISLAND

2 NOVEMBER–22 DECEMBER 1751

> "Sweet is the Air, and mild, and pure; no Damps,
> No Fogs, no subterranean Blasts infect
> Her healthy Sons . . ."[1]

With these words, native poet Nathaniel Weekes lauded Barbados's climate, which was believed to be particularly therapeutic for respiratory complaints. Welsh naturalist Griffith Hughes described Barbados as healthful due to the purifying nature of the trade winds sweeping the island.[2] Hughes gained fame with the 1750 publication of *The Natural History of Barbados*, in which he examined myriad topics—notably animals, plants, vegetables, fruit, marine life, and diseases. Washington may have encountered the book just prior to leaving Virginia; the subscriber list includes many well-known Virginians, among them Lawrence Washington's father-in-law, William Fairfax. Barbados resident James Carter, with whom the Washingtons stayed while looking for their own lodging on the island, also was a subscriber. Washington echoed Hughes's assessment of the island's salutary influence in his substantive diary entry for 22 Dec., noting that it was apparent "in the florid countenances of the Country Gentle[me]n and its said they live to great ages where they are not intemperate."

A Map of the Island of Barbados, Drawn from an Actual Survey, and from the Observations of the Revd. Mr. Griffith Hughes, engraving by Thomas Jefferys, in Griffith Hughes, *The Natural History of Barbados*, London, 1750. (Courtesy of the John Carter Brown Library at Brown University)

The Island

Twenty-one miles long and fourteen miles wide, Barbados is the easternmost Caribbean island. It became part of the British empire in 1627 and did not gain independence until the twentieth century. Robert Poole (1707 or 1708–1752), an English physician and theological writer, described the island topography during his 1748–49 visit as "pleasingly variegated with Ground rising and falling; none very high, nor any extremely low."[3]

The Washingtons arrived at Bridgetown, a bustling seaport on the southwestern corner of the island that included roughly 1,200 houses, on 2 Nov. 1751.[4] Its small harbor in Carlisle Bay experienced such high maritime traffic that a British military physician of the late eighteenth century labeled it the "Thames of the West Indies."[5] Washington remarked upon the view of "all the shipping" in Carlisle Bay, but he did not comment on the less attractive elements, including the abundance of sharks (see the entry for 7 Nov.).[6]

THE
NATURAL HISTORY
OF THE
Island of *BARBADOS.*
BOOK III.

"A Prospect of Bridge-Town in the Island of Barbadoes," title page to Book III of Griffith Hughes, *The Natural History of Barbados*, London, 1750. (Beinecke Rare Book and Manuscript Library, Yale University)

Most of the people in Barbados at the time of the Washingtons' visit were enslaved. According to a 1748 census, the population comprised 15,252 white colonists and 47,132 slaves, meaning free white colonists accounted for just under a quarter of the total population.[7] Poor whites greatly outnumbered large landowners. By contrast, more than half of Virginia's population in 1750 were free whites.[8] Clearly, Washington had never experienced such a racial disparity.

Poole described the white inhabitants of Barbados as "very courteous, humane, and complaisant to Strangers."[9] He noted that they were "thinly clad," dressed principally in "a Linnen Banyan, with thin Caps, hardly any to be seen with Wigs." Poole contrasted the appearance of the "many Blacks, which, for the most Part, have no more Covering on than what Decency requires to cover their Nakedness, being provided with neither Shirt, Shoe nor Stocking, and many of the Children are quite naked: Yet there are a few well-looking Blacks, and neatly habited; but these are said to be kept as Women of Pleasure."[10]

Sugar dominated agriculture in Barbados, and windmills for grinding sugarcane covered the island. Sugar cultivation and production was back-breaking work, and as its

Inset detail of *A New & Exact Map of the Island of Barbadoes in America According to an Actual & Accurate Survey Made in the Years 1717 and 1721 . . .* by William Mayo, 1722, showing a windmill for grinding sugarcane. (Courtesy of the John Carter Brown Library at Brown University)

primary crop shifted from tobacco to sugarcane in the mid-seventeenth century, Barbados became the first British colony to replace indentured servants with African slaves to make up the majority of its work force. The island gained a reputation as a harsh environment for laborers.[11] Poole reflected that "[t]he many Miseries these poor Slaves are subject to, can't but excite Compassion in every considering Mind." Describing the "State of Slavery for Life" as "a shocking Circumstance to a generous Nature," he detailed the experience of Barbadian slaves as "not only exposed daily to the Stroke of the Scourge, but also to Hunger, and to be in want of all Things; hence the Miseries they are liable to suffer are inexpressible. They are drove like Beasts from Place to Place, and frequently are used with far less Compassion."[12]

Sugar cultivation monopolized available land.[13] To fulfill other needs, residents relied on imports of such necessities as livestock, foodstuffs, and lumber, many of which Virginians supplied. In return, Virginians imported slaves from the island. The economic connections between the colonies led some Barbadians to migrate to Virginia to secure more accessible land. These West Indian immigrants brought elements of Caribbean culture—including knowledge of sugar production and harsher attitudes toward slavery[14]—which Washington likely encountered prior to his visit.

Barbados was divided into eleven parishes by the Church of England—the state religion in the British colony—and these served also as political divisions. Each parish was governed by an elected vestry of sixteen landowning men, who levied taxes and administered local civil and ecclesiastical matters.[15] The island's overall colonial government was established in the mid-seventeenth century as a tripartite system with a governor, an advisory Council, and a legislative House of Assembly. Appointed by the Crown, the governor represented the interests of the British empire on the island. Twelve individuals recommended by the governor and approved by the Crown comprised the Council, which advised and monitored the governor. Each of the island's eleven parishes sent two representatives to the Assembly. The right to vote for Assembly members (and for parish vestries) was restricted to white Christian men who were over twenty-one years old, were born in Barbados or were naturalized British subjects, and owned at least ten acres of land or a house worth at least £10. The Assembly introduced all financial law and exercised meaningful economic power.[16]

Sugar planters ruled Barbados. Leading families that traced their ancestry to the frontier years of the 1630s and 1640s owned large plantations and dominated the Assembly, the Council, and civic institutions, tailoring custom and law to protect their supremacy. Less influential families ran smaller farms and lived mainly in the southern and northern ends of the island, where the land was less suited to sugar cultivation.[17]

On 10 Nov. and 15 Dec. 1751, Washington recorded in his diary that he had attended services. The Church of England predominated on Barbados, and Quakers and Jews also lived and worshipped there.[18] Slaves often practiced Obeah, a religious tradition prevalent among the West African diaspora, although Anglican missionaries made attempts to convert practitioners to Christianity. In 1710, Christopher Codrington left two sugar estates in St. John Parish to the Society for the Propagation of the Gospel in Foreign Parts, an Anglican group that pursued missionary endeavors and held that slaves had souls. Planters—who viewed slaves as property—feared the eventual result would be wholesale emancipation.[19]

Because of its strategic location and economic value to the British empire, Barbados was heavily fortified with fixed works. According to a 1736 account of the military strength of the British West Indies, the island was equipped with "twenty-two castles and forts and twenty-six batteries mounted with 463 guns." A provincial military manned the forts and secured the island against attack from foreign adversaries, which never materialized.[20] The militia also functioned as a police force that protected against internal threats, including slave revolts. Barbadian colonial law required a soldier for every twenty acres of land, and a horse for every hundred acres.[21] In 1751 the militia numbered roughly 4,500 men, including mounted and foot regiments, as well as a life guard unit—a cavalry outfit that served as the governor's personal escort. Indentured servants and men who owned little or no land formed the rank and file, while officers belonged to the landed gentry.[22]

Island Culture and Entertainment

Washington enjoyed elite leisure opportunities on Barbados. He and Lawrence dined on 9 Nov. with the Beefsteak and Tripe Club, which modeled itself on a similarly named English social group, founded in London in 1735, whose members met for beefsteak dinners on Saturdays and proclaimed as their motto "Beef and Liberty." At this meal,

George enjoyed fruits both familiar and new. He likely had tasted apples and pomegranates in Virginia, and possibly he had encountered oranges and lemons, which were grown in some Virginia greenhouses, but tropical fruits such as the guava, granadilla (passion fruit), and sapodilla were new experiences for him. He also noted "forbidden fruit," another name for the grapefruit, which most likely originated in Barbados as a cross between the sweet orange and the pomelo, or shaddock.[23]

He attended the annual celebration of Guy Fawkes Day, a remembrance of the failed attempt by Catholic conspirators to blow up the Houses of Parliament and assassinate the British king in 1605, an event often referred to as the Gunpowder Plot or the Gunpowder Treason Plot. (The Council of Barbados minutes for 5 Nov. 1684 include the first mention of a "gunpowder-treason day" on the island.) Celebrants typically marked the event with fireworks, bonfires, and the burning of effigies. Years after his Barbados visit, while serving as commanding general of the Continental Army, Washington would condemn such festivities for diplomatic reasons; in the general orders for 5 Nov. 1775, he decried observance of the anniversary on grounds that it would insult French-Canadian Catholics who supported the American cause.[24]

The arts expanded in Barbados over the first half of the eighteenth century, as the island grew more cosmopolitan. The first newspaper in the eastern Caribbean islands, the *Barbados Gazette*, was printed by Samuel Keimer, who previously had employed Benjamin Franklin in Philadelphia.[25] Among the many poems and excerpts from plays published in the *Gazette* in the 1730s is the "Prologue made to the *Royal Convert*," which begins by imagining the nine Muses, "*New-Comers* to this Hospitable Isle," pleased to see the arts blossoming on Barbados:

> On Azure Skies the *Nine*, transported, gaze,
> To view their God with brighter Beauties blaze.
> *Here*, each Attempt to please, has found Success;
> The *Dance*, the *Concert*, and the *Courtly Dress*.[26]

Dancing had become a common amusement by the time of the Washingtons' visit, and Lawrence wrote to Thomas Fairfax in December 1751: "We have no kind of bodily diversions but dancing."[27]

Washington's stay in Barbados also included his earliest known attendance at the theater. On 14 Nov. he saw *The London Merchant; or, the History of George Barnwell*, written by George Lillo (1693–1739) and first published in 1731. The play is a morality tale aimed at young men; its protagonist, young apprentice George Barnwell, falls prey to Millwood, a scheming temptress who persuades him not only to steal from his honorable master but also to murder his rich uncle. Overwhelmed with guilt, Barnwell is turned over to the law and condemned to the gallows along with Millwood. Barnwell expresses remorse and dies in peace; Millwood's life ends in fear and defiance.

The Barbadoes Mulatto Girl, stipple engraving and etching by Agostino Brunias, 1779. (Yale Center for British Art, Paul Mellon Collection)

The island elite prided themselves, perhaps somewhat facetiously, on their fashion sense: "Barbadian Married Men" boasted to their female counterparts that "We could shew by undoubted Proofs, that we surpass all the Nations in the World in the Size and Cock of our Hats, whether you regard the terrible, or the languishing Style; that our Ruffles are more exactly plaited than they are in *London*, or *Paris*."[28] In his 22 Dec. summary of his time on the island, Washington noted the "very agreeable" ladies, but worried that their affectation of the island's African-inflected cultural mores—known as creolization—diminished their status as Europeans. Some elite white women on Barbados may have emulated the head wraps worn by slave women in the West Indies, and they certainly took on some African or creole speech patterns. One island visitor described white women as using "the Negro Brogue," and the "Barbadian Batchelors" in the *Barbados Gazette* for 30 Sept. 1732 accused white Barbadian women of "several great *Foibles*, such as valuing yourselves too much on your Negroes, lisping their Language."[29] Washington later would advocate the physical separation of whites from slaves, lest the latter influence the former. Writing to his farm manager William Pearce on 16 Nov. 1794, he noted that a Scottish craftsman at Mount Vernon should have "been kept as seperate, and as distinct as possible from the Negros."[30]

Smallpox

After the Washington brothers landed in Bridgetown, they quickly sought accommodations in the countryside. Many believed the Barbados climate therapeutic for those suffering from respiratory afflictions, but Bridgetown had a reputation for sickness, and it was there that Washington contracted smallpox. As the average incubation period lasted from ten to fourteen days, however, he was unaware of his misfortune for almost two weeks. The infection likely occurred on 3 Nov. when the brothers dined at the house of Gedney Clarke Sr. while "smallpox was in his family." He recorded being "strongly attacked" by the disease in his 16 Nov. diary entry. Clarke's physician friend John Lanahan (1699–1762) attended Washington throughout his twenty-five-day bout of the disease. If, as is likely, his experience followed the typical pattern, his first symptoms were mild and mimicked a less severe illness, with the signature rash appearing within a few days and spreading quickly. His only recourse would have been to follow his doctor's prescribed treatment, which included bleeding, purging, and the use of anti-inflammatory medicines.[31]

His recovery from the disease granted him lifetime immunity, which served him well during his military career. Smallpox ran rampant during the Revolutionary War. European soldiers brought the disease with them, and colonial troops traveling longer distances than ever before contracted it from new people they encountered in new environments. Inoculation, which curbed general outbreaks, involved implanting a live smallpox variola into the patient's skin to induce a milder form of the disease and subsequent immunity.[32] A concerned Washington wrote to Maj. Gen. Horatio Gates in early February 1777: "I am much at a loss what Step to take to prevent the spreading of the smallpox; should We innoculate generally, the Enemy, knowing it, will certainly take Advantage of our Situation."[33] Ultimately, he required all new recruits to be inoculated before joining the Continental Army.

Washington documented varying impressions of Barbados. On 4 Nov., two days after arriving, he raved about the "beautiful prospects" of the island and "fields of Cain, Corn, Fruit Trees, &c. in a delightful Green." Just a few days later, he was frustrated at Lawrence's obligation to pay the "extravagantly dear" cost of lodging. As he took leave of the island, he composed by far the longest entry in the Barbados diary. His 22 Dec. commentary moves nimbly among subjects, from the island's government, geography, and agriculture to its people, economy, and military. Whether Washington wrote it all on 22 Dec. or took a few days is hard to determine. The scope of his observations and reflections demonstrates his lifelong talent for absorbing, distilling, analyzing, and retaining information in often astonishing detail. Years later, he would admit to a preference for written communication so that he could "digest every matter and thing at my leizure"[34]—a tendency that would prove invaluable, especially during the Revolutionary War.

The young man had observed fortifications, tried new foods, attended what may have been his first play, and become acquainted with a slave-based economy very different from that of his own home colony. He had dined with powerful politicians, seen women in unfamiliar dress, and spent time with elite planters and judges. In the end, he departed the island without his brother. The celebrated Barbados climate had failed to cure Lawrence's ailment.

---

1. Nathaniel Weekes, *Barbados: A Poem* (London, 1754), 15.
2. See G. Hughes, *Natural History of Barbados*, 24–25.
3. Poole, *Beneficent Bee: or, Traveller's Companion*, 207.
4. Ibid., 286. Poole estimated the number of houses in Bridgetown.
5. Pinckard, *Notes on the West Indies*, 1:443; see also Draper, "Tropical Metropolis," 300.
6. Sharks were lured, in particular, by the dead bodies of diseased slaves thrown overboard (see G. Hughes, *Natural History of Barbados*, 312).
7. See Molen, "Population and Social Patterns in Barbados," 289. Griffith Hughes estimated the black population in 1750 at between 65,000 and 70,000 (*Natural History of Barbados*, 14).
8. See *Historical Statistics of the United States: Colonial Times to 1970, Bicentennial Edition* (2 parts; Washington, D.C., 1975), 2:1168.
9. Poole, *Beneficent Bee: or, Traveller's Companion*, 288.
10. Ibid., 208. A *banian* was a loose shirt or gown worn especially by Hindu traders, who also were called banians.
11. See Hatfield, *Atlantic Virginia*, 140, and Molen, "Population and Social Patterns in Barbados," 287–88. For greater context on slavery and the transatlantic economy, see Dunn, *Sugar and Slaves*.
12. Poole, *Beneficent Bee: or, Traveller's Companion*, 253.
13. See Keagy, "Poor Whites of Barbados," 10.
14. See Hatfield, *Atlantic Virginia*, 140–41.
15. See, for example, Molen, "Population and Social Patterns in Barbados," 291; Watson, *Civilised Island, Barbados*, 8–9; and Schomburgk, *History of Barbados*, 92–93.
16. See Watson, *Civilised Island, Barbados*, 5–8. For a contemporary description of the government of Barbados, see Poole, *Beneficent Bee: or, Traveller's Companion*, 215–16.

17. See Hilary McD. Beckles, *A History of Barbados: From Amerindian Settlement to Caribbean Single Market* (Cambridge, England, 2006), 54, 57.

18. For more information on religion in Barbados, see Larry Dale Gragg, *The Quaker Community on Barbados: Challenging the Culture of the Planter Class* (Columbia, Mo., 2009); Richard L. Kagan and Philip D. Morgan, eds., *Atlantic Diasporas: Jews, Conversos, and Crypto-Jews in the Age of Mercantilism, 1500–1800* (Baltimore, 2009); and Carla Gardina Pestana, *Protestant Empire: Religion and the Making of the British Atlantic World* (Philadelphia, 2009).

19. See Klingberg, Introduction to *Codrington Chronicle*, 4–6; McCulloch and Schutz, "Noble and Generous Benefaction of Codrington," 15–19; Bennett, *Bondsmen and Bishops*, especially 75–87; and Schomburgk, *History of Barbados*, 93–94.

20. See Schomburgk, *History of Barbados*, 192–95.

21. See Hall, *Acts, Passed in the Island of Barbados*, 138–39.

22. See Jerome S. Handler, "Freedmen and Slaves in the Barbados Militia," *Journal of Caribbean History* 19 (1984): 2–4.

23. See J. Kumamoto et al., "Mystery of the Forbidden Fruit: Historical Epilogue on the Origin of the Grapefruit, *Citrus paradisi* (Rutaceae)," *Economic Botany* 41 (1987): 97–107.

24. See *PGW-Revolutionary* 2:300.

25. See Arthur, *Caribbean Treasure*, 24–31.

26. *Barbados Gazette* for 16 Aug. 1732, in Arthur, *Caribbean Treasure*, 52–53.

27. See Appendix C. Lawrence Washington continued ominously that dancing "frequently produces yellow fever."

28. *Barbados Gazette* for 7 Oct. 1732, in Arthur, *Caribbean Treasure*, 60, 62.

29. Poole, *Beneficent Bee: or, Traveller's Companion*, 288; *Barbados Gazette* for 30 Sept. 1732, in Arthur, *Caribbean Treasure*, 56.

30. *PGW-Presidential* 17:166.

31. See Hillary, *Small-Pox*; Fox et al., *Practical Treatise on Smallpox*; and Fenn, *Pox Americana*.

32. Ibid.

33. GW to Horatio Gates, 5–6 Feb. 1777, in *PGW-Revolutionary* 8:248.

34. GW to Arthur St. Clair, 4 Oct. 1779 (*PGW-Revolutionary* 22:619). See also Ferraro, "Washington's Mind," 542–57.

THE DIARY ENTRIES

◆

Sunday, 3 November 1751

<*November* [3d], 1751.[1]—This morning received a card from Major Clarke, welcoming us to Barbadoes, with an invitation to breakfast and dine with him.[2] We went,—myself with some reluctance, as the smallpox was in his family.[3] We were received in the most kind and friendly manner by him. Mrs. Clarke was much indisposed, insomuch that we had not the pleasure of her company, but in her place officiated Miss Roberts, her niece, and an agreeable young lady.[4] After drinking tea we were again invited to Mr. Carter's, and desired to make his house ours till we could provide lodgings agreeable to our wishes, which offer we accepted.>[5]

1. Because a manuscript page is missing, this entry and part of the one for 4 Nov. are taken from Sparks, *Writings*, 2:424. GW recorded incorrect dates for the entries between 5–8 and 10–16 Nov.—erroneously ahead by one calendar day—and presumably did the same for 3 and 4 Nov., as is reflected in Sparks's misdating of the early entries.

2. The invitation has not been found. For biographical information on Gedney Clarke Sr., who was Ann Fairfax Washington's uncle by marriage, see p. xli in the introduction to this volume.

3. Mary Fleurian (b. 1708), Clarke's wife, may have been the afflicted individual. For more on smallpox, see p. 57 in the introductory essay to this part of the diary.

4. Elizabeth Roberts was Mary Fleurian Clarke's niece.

5. James Carter (1712–1753), a relative of the wealthy and prominent Virginia Carters, served on the Barbados Council in the 1740s and was appointed chief justice of Grand Sessions in 1749. Carter owned Spring Plantation in St. Thomas Parish and a plantation in Christ Church Parish.

Monday, 4 November 1751

<[4]*th*.[1]—Early this morning came Dr. Hilary, an eminent physician recommended by Major Clarke, to pass his opinion on my brother's disorder, which he did in a favorable light, giving great assurances that it was not so fixed but that a cure might be effectually made.[2] In the cool of the evening we rode out accompanied by Mr. Carter to seek lodgings in the country, as the Doctor advised,> And[3] was perfectly rav<ished by>[4] the beautiful prospects wh<ich on> every side presented to our view The fields of Cain, Corn, Fruit Trees, &c. in a delightful Green. We return'd without accomplis<h>ing our intentions.

1. See the entry for 3 Nov., n.1.
2. For biographical information on William Hillary, see p. xl in the "In Barbados" section of the introduction.
3. Transcription from the manuscript resumes with this word.
4. For a less plausible rendering—"enraptured with"—see Sparks, *Writings*, 2:424.

Tuesday, 5 November 1751

Tuesday [5]th[1]

At Mr Carter's imploying ourselves in Writg Letters, to be carried by the Chooner Fredericksburg; Captn Robinson to Virginia.[2] receiv'd a Card from Majr Clarke wherein our companys were desir'd to Dinner to morrow & myself an invitation from Mrs Clarke & Miss Robts to come & see the Serpts fir'd being Gun P[owder] T[reason].[3] I had the pleasure of seeing Mrs C[l]ark<e>.[4]

1. GW mistakenly wrote "6" for the date.

2. Cornelius Robertson captained the 80-ton schooner *Fredericksburg*, which cleared Port Rappahannock for Barbados on 2 or 3 Sept. with a cargo of corn, oats, shingles, and British linen. Given bond on 8 Nov. in Barbados, the *Fredericksburg* soon sailed, presumably for Virginia and possibly carrying the barrel of limes that GW bought on 9 Nov. for his brother-in-law Fielding Lewis (see LC-Ledger A, folio 8, left). During voyages between Virginia and Barbados in 1752, the *Fredericksburg* carried cargo that included Barbadian rum and "35 Negroes" (see the *Virginia Gazette* [Williamsburg] for 3 Oct. 1751, and 7 and 14 Aug. 1752; P.R.O.: C.O. 5/1444, folios 118 and 122 and the verso to each, Naval Office Shipping Lists for Virginia).

3. GW is referring to fireworks that commemorated the Gunpowder Plot, also known as Guy Fawkes Day. For more information on the celebration, see p. 56 in the introductory essay to this part of the diary.

4. Although GW might have written "h" as the second letter in this name, context strongly suggests the wife of Gedney Clarke Sr. (see the entry for 3 Nov.). For a dubious conclusion that GW wrote "Mr. Church" instead, see Fitzpatrick, *Diaries*, 1:23.

Wednesday, 6 November 1751

View of Carlisle Bay, Barbados, with Ships and Boat, watercolor by Paul Sandby, c.1820. (Yale Center for British Art, Paul Mellon Collection)

<Wednesd>ay [6]th[1]

Dined at Majr Clarkes; and by him was introduced to the Surveyor Genl[2] [&] Judges, Finley & Hacket;[3] who likewise din'd there: in the Evening they complaisantly accompanied us in another excursion in the Country to choose such lodgings as most suited; we pitched on the house of Captn ~~Crawford~~ Croftan commander of James Fort;[4] he was desir'd to come to Town next day to propose his terms. We return'd by way of Needham's fort & was introduced to the Captn thereof, a ~~good~~ Genteel pretty < > man.[5] Sup'd and spent t<he> Evening at Majr C[l]arke with the Gentlemen before mentioned.

1. GW mistakenly wrote "7" for the date.

2. William Patterson (Paterson) served from 1746 to 1759 as the surveyor general for Antigua, Barbados, the Leeward Islands, and Bermuda.

3. Thomas Finlay (Findlay; d. 1760), a native of Scotland, worked as clerk of the General Assembly of Barbados, 1743–44.

"Hacket" may refer to either Othinil (Othniel; d. 1761) or Nathaniel Haggatt, lawyers living in Barbados at the time. A section of the island east of Bridgetown in St. Michael Parish is known as "Haggatt Hall."

4. Militia officer Richard Crofton's home near James Fort was a mile from Bridgetown at the northern end of Carlisle Bay.

5. GW is referring to Charles Fort at Needham's Point. That structure, built in 1650, stood in Bridgetown at the southern end of Carlisle Bay. Militia captain George John Petrie most likely commanded Charles Fort during GW's visit.

A Panoramic View of Carlisle Bay, Barbados, with Cottages and Ships, watercolor by Paul Sandby, c.1820. (Yale Center for British Art, Paul Mellon Collection)

Thursday, 7 November 1751

Thursday [7]th[1]

Came Captn Croftan ~~Crawford~~ with his proposals which tho extravagantly dear my Brother was oblig'd to give £15 pr Month is his charge exclusive of Liquors[2] & washing which we find. in the Evening we remov'd some of our things up and ourselves. its very pleasantly situated p[r]etty < >[3] the Sea and abt a mile from Town the prospect is extensive by Land and ~~agreeable both by Land~~ pleasant by Sea as we command the prospect of Carlyle Bay & all the shipping in such manner that none can go in or out without being open to our view.

1. GW mistakenly wrote "8" for the date.
2. "Liquors" refers to any liquid, not just alcohol.
3. GW likely wrote a word or phrase in this space related to proximity.

Friday, 8 November 1751

Fryday [8]th[1]

We receivd a Card from Majr Clarke inviting us to dine with him at Judge Maynards on the Morrow[2] he had a right to ask being a Member of the Club call'd the Beefstake & tripe instituted by himself.[3]

1. GW mistakenly wrote "9" for the date.

2. The invitation has not been found. GW gave Maynard various titles: Judge, Colonel, Mr., and "Satyr" or "Satus" (see the entry for 9 Nov.). Many Maynards lived on the island, but this probably was William Maynard (d. 1765), a member of the General Assembly and owner of Black Rock Plantation in St. Thomas Parish, on the border with the parishes of St. James and St. Michael. Other possibilities include Jonas Maynard (d. 1781), who was a member of the Assembly for St. Michael Parish; John Maynard, a Bridgetown attorney; and Thomas Maynard (d. 1784), who resided in St. Thomas Parish.

3. For information about the Beefsteak and Tripe Club, see p. 55 in the introductory essay to this part of the diary.

Saturday, 9 November 1751

<Saturday 9th>[1]

[. . .] the Judges Maynard < > Robt Warren Esqr.[2] & Captn Petr<ie> (the Commander of Needhams Fort) We were Genteely receivd by ~~Judge~~ Sat<yr>[3] Maynard & ~~his~~ Lady and agreeably entertain'd by the Company they have a meeting every saturday this being Colo. Maynards After Dinner was the greatest Collection of Fruits I have yet seen set on the Table there was the Granadella the Sappadilla Pomgranate Sweet Orange Water Lemmon forbidden Fruit apples Guaba's &ca &ca &ca.[4] We receivd invitations from every Gentleman there & one <from Jud>ge Jenkin's who also <was> there tho not one of their <~~Club~~>Mem[be]rs.[5] Mr Warren desir'd Majr Clarke to shew us the way to his house; Mr Hack[e]t insisted on our coming Saturday next to his ~~house~~ being his Day to treat with Beef Stake & tripe but above all the invitation of Mr Maynard was the most kind and friendly he desir'd and even insisted as well as his Lady on our coming to spend some Weeks with him and promis'd nothing shoud be wanting ~~in him~~ to render our stay agreeable my Br[other] promis'd he wou'd as soon as he was a Little disengagd from the D[octo]rs. We return'd and by th< > was invited to Dine at M<ajor> Clarke's the next Day by Himself.

1. The 9 Nov. entry is written on a new sheet of paper. Presumably one leaf (likely no more) is missing between this entry and the one for 8 Nov. (see also Toner, *Daily Journal*, 49–50).

2. Robert Warren (d. 1755) had been the clerk of the General Assembly and register in Chancery. He lived in St. Michael Parish approximately five miles from GW's lodgings.

3. Text below obscures the last two letters. "Satyr" was a playful title for the leader of a party. An earlier editor rendered this word as "Satus" (Toner, *Daily Journal*, 49), which is Latin for "native." Another editor was surely mistaken to transcribe "Satuo," though he supported Toner's reading in annotation (Fitzpatrick, *Diaries*, 1:24).

4. For more information on the fruits that GW sampled in Barbados, see p. 55 in the introductory essay to this part of the diary.

5. Edmund Jenkins (died c.1765) resided in Bridgetown and served as chief judge of St. James Parish in 1752.

The George Washington House, Bridgetown, Barbados, the brothers' lodging during their stay on the island. The house has been considerably altered and enlarged since 1751. (Photograph by Alicia K. Anderson)

Sunday, 10 November 1751

Sunday 1[0]th[1]

Dressed in order for Church but got to town two Late din'd at Majr Clarkes with the S[urveyor] G[eneral] ~~and~~ went to Evening Service and return'd to ~~evening Service~~our Lodgings ~~in the Evening a~~[f]~~terwards.~~[2]

1. GW mistakenly wrote "11" for the date.

2. GW most likely attended St. Michael's church in Bridgetown due to its proximity to the brothers' lodgings. Originally consecrated in 1665, the church impressed a visitor on Christmas Day 1749: "This is a pretty large Church . . . . It is furnished with Galleries on each Side, and has a small Organ. The Roof is ceiled; and the Body of the Church, with the Galleries, will suffice to hold a large Congregation. Its Windows, except those about the Communion, are generally unglaized. The Governor's Pew is conveniently situated for hearing: It is large, lined with red, and furnished with an Elbow-Chair in the Middle, which is also lined in the same Manner" (Poole, *Beneficent Bee: or, Traveller's Companion*, 217). The church was rebuilt after a hurricane in 1780 and renamed the Cathedral Church of Saint Michael and All Angels.

Monday, 11 November 1751

Munday 1[1]th[1]

receiv'd an afternoon Visit from Captn Petrie and an invitation to dine with him the next Day.

1. GW mistakenly wrote "12" for the date.

Tuesday, 12 November 1751

<Tuesda>y 1[2]th[1]

Dined at the Fort[2] with some Ladys its pretty strongly fortifyed and mounts about 36 Guns within the fortifi[catio]n but 2 facine Batterys m[oun]t 5< >.[3]

1. GW mistakenly wrote "13" for the date.
2. GW is referring to Charles Fort.
3. Although part of the second numeral is now missing, previous editors have read the number as "51," which was the total cannon mounted within the main fort and its defenses, according to a contemporary depiction of the work (see *Plan of Charles Fort, Barbados, and the two Fascine Batteries adjoining, from an actual survey of 1748* at the P.R.O.; see also Toner, *Daily Journal*, 52, and Fitzpatrick, *Diaries*, 1:25).

George Barnwell, frontispiece to George Lillo, *The London Merchant: Or, the History of George Barnwell. A Tragedy*, London, 1776. (Courtesy of Lynn A. Price)

Wednesday, 13 November 1751

Wednesday 1[3]th[1]

At our Lodgings.

1. GW mistakenly wrote "14" for the date.

Thursday, 14 November 1751

Thursday 1[4][1]

Was treated with a play ticket by Mr Carter to see the Tragedy of George Barnwell acted: the charactar of Barnwell and several others was said to be well perform'd there was ~~a band of~~ Musick a Dapted and regularly conducted by Mr [ ].[2]

1. GW mistakenly wrote "15" for the date.

2. For GW's experience watching a performance of George Lillo's ***The London Merchant; or, the History of George Barnwell***, a morality play for young men dating from 1731, see p. 57 in the introductory essay to this part of the diary.

Friday, 15 November 1751

Fryday 1[5]th[1]

Mr Gr~~ah~~æme <late one>[2] of the Master's of the College of Virginia ~~came to Visit us~~ paid us a Mornings Visit and invit<ed> us to dine with Judge Græme his Br[other] on Sunday:[3] din'd this Day at Majr Clarke's.

1. GW mistakenly wrote "16" for the date.

2. The letters "la" here come from Toner, *Daily Journal*, 52, and Fitzpatrick, *Diaries*, 1:25.

3. John Græme (d. 1755) of London taught natural philosophy and mathematics at the College of William and Mary until 1749. Græme had surveyed William Fairfax's landholdings in Virginia during the 1730s, as GW did a decade or so later.

George Græme (died c.1755), John's brother, was a member of the Barbados General Assembly for Christ Church Parish. GW dined at his home on 15 December.

Saturday, 16 November 1751

Saturday 1[6]th[1]

Was strongly attac<k>ed with the small Pox: Sent for Dr Lanahan[2] whose attendance was very constant till my recovery and going out which was not 'till thursday the 12th of December.[3]

1. GW mistakenly wrote "17" for the date.

2. John Lanahan was a physician and friend of the senior Gedney Clarke.

3. GW recorded nothing in his diary for the next twenty-five days. For more on his experience with smallpox, see p. 57 in the introductory essay to this part of the diary.

Thursday, 12 December 1751

<Thursday> December 12th

Went to Town visited Majr Clarke's Family (who ~~was so~~ kindly ~~several times to~~ visited me in my illness and contributed all they cou'd in sendg me the necessary's required in that disorder) and dined with Majr Gasken, a half Br[other] to Mrs Clarke:[1] On Munday last began the Grand sescions and this Day brought on the Tryal of Colo. Chaunack a Man of oppulent fortune ~~but~~And infamous Charactar he was indicted for commiting a rape on his servant Maid and was brought in Guiltless and sav'd by one single Evidence on<ly > was generally reckone<d > Suborn'd.[2]

1. John Gaskin (1720–1779) likely was related to the Gascoigne family from Yorkshire, England. The Gascoignes had strong ties with the Clarke family in England, Virginia, and Barbados.

2. The acquitted man most likely was Benjamin Charnock (1698–1783) of St. James Parish. The "servant Maid" likely was white, because black slaves under Barbados law had no legal rights and could not bring a rape case to court. For more information on slaves and the court system in Barbados, see Handler, "Custom and law," 13, and Palmer, *A Rule of Law*, 43, 119, 145. See also Hall, *Acts, Passed in the Island of Barbados*, 112–13, 158.

Friday, 13 December 1751

Fryday 13th

Spent at our Lodging<s>.

Saturday, 14 December 1751

Saturday 14th

My Br[other] dined at Needham's myself at Maj<or> Clarkes.

Sunday, 15 December 1751

Sunday 15th:

Dined with Judge Græme after returning from Christ Church.[1]

1. Christ Church overlooks Oistin's Bay, approximately five miles from where GW was lodging. A visitor in 1749 described the interior of the building: "It is a neat Church, high roofed, well ceiled, and furnished with an Organ, which is said to be the best in *America*. The Altar is decorated with the ten Commandments, Lord's Prayer, and Creed; with *Moses* and *Aaron*, extremely well done, placed at each Side, which compleats its Decoration. The Rails round the Altar are not very neat or regular" (Poole, *Beneficent Bee: or, Traveller's Companion*, 293). A hurricane destroyed the church in 1780.

For an invitation to dine at George Græme's home, see the entry for 15 November. The same earlier visitor who described Christ Church commented on Græme's situation being "a very pleasant one. It stands high, at no great Distance from the Sea, and commands a noble Prospect." He considered the "Garden" to be "one of the best I have seen in the island" (Poole, *Beneficent Bee: or, Traveller's Companion*, 293).

Monday, 16 December 1751

Munday 16th

Dined at Needham<'s> Fort with Captn Petrie.

Tuesday, 17 December 1751

<Tuesday 1>[7]th[1]

Dined at Majr Clark<e's> with comodore Hobourn[,] Governr Pursel G[overno]r of Totola[,] General Barrack & many others.[2]

1. Again losing track of the days, GW mistakenly wrote "<1>6" for the date (see the entry for 3 Nov., n.1). He did not record the correct date again until his entry for 21 December.

2. Francis Holburne (Holbourn; 1704–1771), a British naval officer, became commander in chief of the Leeward Islands in 1748.

James Purcell (d. 1759) served as the president of the British Virgin Islands, 1750–51. John Purcell (d. 1771), James's brother, served in the same post 1751–71. The president (referred to as lieutenant governor starting in 1751) was headquartered on the island of Tortola.

"General Barrack" may have been William Barwick (d. 1756), who owned Pine Plantation in St. Michael Parish and served on the Barbados Council.

Wednesday, 18 December 1751

Wednesday 1[8]th[1]

Dined with Messrs Stephenson's Merchts.[2]

1. GW mistakenly wrote "17" for the date.

2. Thomas Stevenson (Stephenson; d. 1763) conducted a merchant business with his sons on Barbados and other West Indian islands. He owned Pool Plantation, a sugar estate in St. John Parish, and variously held posts as the provost marshal general of Barbados, surveyor general, and deputy sergeant at arms. As an astronomer, Stevenson studied Halley's Comet.

Thursday, 19 December 1751

Thursday 1[9][1]

Provided my Sea Store[2] & dined with ~~Ca~~<~~p~~>Mr Cart<e>r.

1. GW mistakenly wrote "18" for the date.

2. GW is referring to his supplies, such as food, which he distinguished from his clothes (see the entry for 20 Dec.).

Friday, 20 December 1751

Fryday [20]th[1]

Got my Clothes Store &c. on board the Industry Captn John Saunders for Virginia.[2]

1. GW mistakenly wrote "19" for the date.

2. For information about the ***Industry***, see p. 81 in the introductory essay to "The Return Voyage."

Saturday, 21 December 1751

Saturday 21st

At my Lodging<s with> my Brother.

Sunday 22d

Took my Leave of my Br[other][1] Majr Clarke &ca & Imbar<ked> in the Industry Captn John Saund<ers> for Virginia wai'd anchor and got out of Carlile Bay abt 12.

The Governer of Barbado's seem<s> to keep a proper State:[2] Lives very retired and at Little expence it is said he is a Gentleman of good Sence As he avoids the Error of his predecessor he gives no handl<e> for complaint but at the same time by declining much familiarity is not overzealously beloved and being deprived of power to < our>s m<eet>[3] with < > &ca.[4] There is sev<eral> regular risings in this Island one above another so that scarcely <a>ny part is deprived of a beautifu<l> Prospect both of Sea & Land and what is contrary to the observatio<n i>n other Countrys is that each <ri>sing is better than the other belo<w>.

There are many delicious Fruits ~~in this~~[5] but as they are particularly describ'd by the Rev<d> Mr Hughs in his Natural hist[or]y <o>f the Island[6] shall say nothing furt<her t>han that the ~~Pine Apple~~ China <O>range is good the Avagado pair is generally most admired tho none pleases my taste as do's the Pine.

The Earth in most parts is extreamely rich & as black as our richest Marsh < > common produce of ca< > Canes is from 40 to 70 polls[7] of Sugar each poll valued at 20/[8] ou<t> of which a third is deducted for expences unless rum sells for 2/ and upwards pr Gallon then it is though the Sugar is near clear. There was many Acres last Year that turn'd out from 140 to 170£ as I was inform'd by credible auth[orit]y tho that was in Ginger & a very extraordinary Yea<r> for the Sail thereof How wonderfu<l> such people shou'd be in debt! & not be able to indulge themselves in all the Luxurys as well as necessarys of Life Yet so it happens Estates are often alienated for debts indeed <a loan bear>ing an Interest of Eigh<t percent is a> great Cancer in an Estate <if> bought at a full Value on Interes<t> but how persons coming to Estates of two, three, and four hundd Acres (which are the largest) can want is most wonderful to Me ⅓ of their Land or nearly generally is in Cane for Harvest the rest is in Young Cane Gunia Corn (which

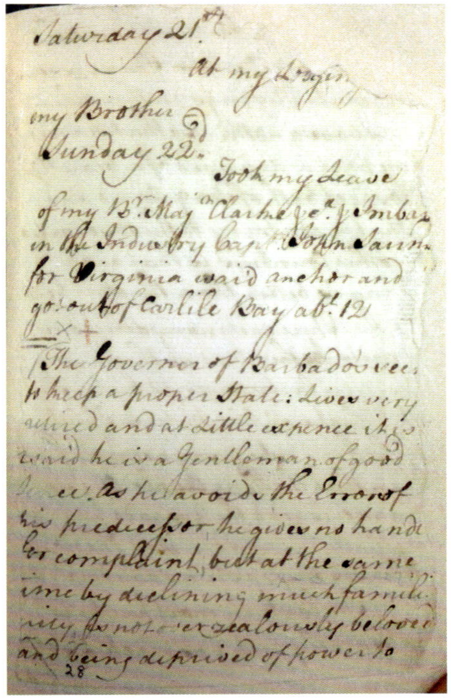

Entries for 21–22 Dec. 1751, George Washington, Diary, 1751–52. (George Washington Papers, Series 1, Exercise Books, Diaries, and Surveys 1745–99, Subseries 1B, Manuscript Division, Library of Congress; photograph by Alicia K. Anderson and Lynn A. Price)

Pineapple as depicted in Richard Ligon, *A True & Exact History Of the Island of Barbadoes . . .*, London, 1673. "[N]one pleases my taste as do's the Pine" (diary entry for 22 Dec. 1751). (Missouri Botanical Garden)

greatly support<s> their Negros) Yams plantens Potatos &c. &ca and some small part left waste for Stock. Their dung the~~ir~~y are very careful in saving, & curious in makg which they do by ~~heaping~~ througing up large heaps of Ear<th> and a Number of Stakes drove ther<e>in sufficient for Sixteen head of Cattle to Stand seperately tied too which they are three Months together tramp<l>[in]g all the trash &ca t< > and then its fit to manu<re the> Ground. Provisions in Genl are very indeferent but much better than the same quantity of pasturage wou'd afford in Virginia The very grass that grows amongst their corn is not Lost but carefully gather'd for provender for their Stoc<k>.

Hospitality & a Genteel behav<ior> is shewn to every gente~~lman~~el Stranger by the Gentlemen Inhab[itan]<ts> Tavorns they have none but in their Towns so that Travellers is oblig'd to go to private houses however the Island being but abt 22 Miles in length & 14 in width preven<ts> their being much infested with them.

The Ladys Generally are very agreeable but by ill custom or wh[ich] < > affect the Negro Style[9] <The hea>lthiness of this Island <is> sufficiently shewn in the florid countenances of the Country Gentle[me]n and its said they live to great ages where they are not intemperate they are however very unhappy in regard to there Officers Fees which are not fixed by any Law they complain particularly of the Provost Marsha<ll> (or Shiref Genl)[10] of the Island Patented at Home and rented at 800£ pr ann<um> Ster[lin]g every other officer is exorbitan<t> in demanding. There are few who may be calld midling people they are either very rich or very poor for by a Law of the Island Every Gent[lema]n is oblig'd to keep a white person for every ten Acres capable of acting in the Malitia and consequently those persons so kept cant but [be] very poor The Numbe<r of militia in> Barbado's is computed < > Thousand (which is more th<an> is in Jamaica & all the other Leewa<rd> Islands)[11] they are well disciplin'd & appointed to their several Station<s> So that ~~in~~upon an allarm every Man is at his post in less than two Hou<rs> They have large Intrenchments cast up where ever its possible for an Enemy to Land and may not (as nature has greatly assis<t>ed) improperly be said to be one entire fortification.

1. Lawrence Washington remained in Barbados before going to Bermuda (see p. xlii in the introduction to this volume and Appendix C).

2. GW probably composed this extended commentary on 22 Dec., but it is possible that he wrote it later.

3. For the previous two words, see Toner, *Daily Journal*, 57, and Fitzpatrick, *Diaries*, 1:27.

4. Henry Grenville (1717–1784) served as governor of Barbados from 1747 to 1753, when he returned to England. Grenville's predecessor, Thomas Robinson (1702 or 1703–1777), resigned in 1747 amid charges of wasteful spending and maladministration (see Schomburgk, *History of Barbados*, 326–27).

5. Written over illegible letters or perhaps a word, this incomplete phrase is treated as struck-out text.

6. For Griffith Hughes and his work *The Natural History of Barbados*, see p. 51 in the introductory essay to this part of the diary.

7. A harvest yields stalks, or "poles," of sugarcane.

8. The slash represents shillings. See the discussion of "Abbreviations, Contractions, and Symbols" in the Editorial Methodology.

9. GW is referring to creolization (see p. 57 in the introductory essay to this part of the diary).

10. Francis Reynolds (d. 1773) served as provost marshal of Barbados between 1741 and 1761. He represented Lancaster, England, as a member of Parliament from 1745 until his death.

11. GW most likely is referring to former indentured servants. By law, these men were permitted to lease a plot of land on a plantation if they agreed to join the militia to fulfill the colony's requirement of one white person for every twenty acres (see Hall, *Acts, Passed in the Island of Barbados*, 139). GW misstated the land requirement. For more on the Barbados militia, see p. 55 in the introductory essay to this part of the diary.

THE RETURN VOYAGE

22 DECEMBER 1751–30 JANUARY 1752

It was noon on 22 Dec. 1751 when George Washington sailed from Bridgetown harbor aboard the brig *Industry*. Two days earlier he had stowed his provisions and other belongings on board. He took leave of new friends and acquaintances that morning. When Washington next saw his brother, all hopes for Lawrence's cure would be gone.

Just three days into the voyage homeward, Christmas Day gave Washington occasion for reflection. As he sailed farther from Barbados and his experiences became memories, a round of Christmas toasts onboard the *Industry* brought "absent friends" to mind, especially the ailing brother who stayed behind for one last attempt at recovery. To round out the day's festivities, he dined on beef and a specially prepared "Irish goose" with his shipmates.

THE *INDUSTRY*

Built in Swansea, Wales, in 1748, the square-sterned vessel *Industry* weighed fifty tons. The brig's owner, Capt. John Saunders (Sandars, Sanders), resided in Bristol, England, and he registered the *Industry* there on 22 March of that year. Previously master of the

York, Saunders made voyages between Bristol and the York River in Virginia during the 1740s.[1] The *Industry* sailed the same route, returning to America by way of Barbados. Given bond at Bristol on 5 Aug. 1751 and at Bridgetown on 19 Nov., the *Industry*—laden with 1,230 gallons of rum and 1,608 pounds of sugar—departed with a crew of seven at the time of Washington's embarkation, arriving at Port York, Va., five tumultuous weeks later. Saunders returned to Bristol on 21 April, taking tobacco, iron, staves, and oars from Virginia.[2]

Peril at Sea

Though he had faced inclement weather on the outbound voyage with Lawrence, young George Washington—now on his own—saw worse conditions on the way home. He wrote no more about fishing or collecting navigational data. The stormy weather undoubtedly impeded such activities.

Washington knew his vulnerability from the outset. He became seasick less than a day into the journey. "Met with a brisk Trade Wind and pretty large Swell wch made the Ship rowl much and me very sick," he noted in his entry for 23 December. Christmas brought temporary respite. He enjoyed the celebratory meal and dined agreeably the next day on "very fine Bristol Tripe." But two weeks later, on 9 Jan., illness plagued him again as the ship's rolling made him "a Criple."

His response to the isolation and danger of the turbulent, five-week passage can be surmised from his terse diary entries. From the "fiery breezes" and sultry heat of the tropics to the thunderstorms and snow of more northerly waters, Washington weathered extremes that likely drove him below deck on a cramped ship. The gales of 24 Dec. "hurried us pass the Leeward Islands." By the 28th, "a sudden change of the Air" produced cloudbursts. Successive squalls drenched the vessel almost daily for the next three weeks. The wind wavered so much on 29 Dec. that "the Vessel often wou'd not lay her course." Experiencing thunder, lightning, rain, and hail, he often described the conditions during these weeks as "violent" (see the entries for 31 Dec., 3 Jan., 9–12 Jan., and 14 Jan.). Pushing back fear, he and the crew sometimes fought the ocean for their lives.

Washington felt distress of a different sort when he realized on 10 Jan. 1752 that someone had stolen money from him in the amount of "16 pistoles." He likely longed for the voyage's end, which came in late January when the pilot boat guided the *Industry* into port at York. He returned to Virginia soil on 30 Jan. and hurried to Williamsburg on an errand to the governor.

Frightening moments at sea surely had etched themselves into Washington's mind. He never took another extended sea voyage, despite many invitations and opportunities after he had secured global fame.[3]

---

1. P.R.O.: C.O. 5/1444, folio 43, Naval Office Shipping Lists for Virginia; Vi: Survey Reports 2100, 2101, 7937, and 8590, Virginia Colonial Records Project.

2. P.R.O.: C.O. 5/1444, folios 43, 44 (verso), Naval Office Shipping Lists for Virginia. Saunders apparently transported goods GW purchased in 1759 (see Invoice from Richard Washington, 20 March 1759, and GW to Richard Washington, 20 Sept. 1759, in *PGW-Colonial* 6:195–96 and 358–59).

3. See Flexner, *Washington*, 51; Callahan, *Washington*, 5; and Chernow, *Washington*, 25, 411.

THE DIARY ENTRIES

◆

MONDAY, 23 DECEMBER 1751

<Monday 23d>[1]

Met with a brisk Trade Wind and pretty large Swell wch made the Ship rowl much and me very sick[2] at 2 P:M: Espyd a Sail in the Latitude of Martineca bearing down for the Island.[3]

1. GW used land time rather than sea time for his entries on the return voyage (for the difference, see p. 9 in the introductory essay to "Sailing to Barbados."
2. This is GW's first reference to suffering from seasickness. Similar conditions, however, likely prompted earlier bouts (see the editorial note for 25–27 Sept. and the entry for 17 Oct.).
3. See the entry for 1 Nov., n.1.

Tuesday, 24 December 1751

Tuesday 24th

A Fresh gale (or what in this part of the World is called a fiery Breeze)[1] hurried us pass the Leeward Islands[2] so the Captn altered his course from No. to NWb<N>.

1. Trade winds and currents, at their strongest in the Caribbean from May to December, caused coastal storms—often during the middle of the day—that blew from the east or southeast. Dead calms typically followed the storms (see Cowley, *Windward Passage*, 15). Lawrence Washington likely knew about these "fiery" breezes from his service in the West Indies under Adm. Edward Vernon, who complained in June 1741 of the "great Interruption" to naval operations caused by "the fiery-breeze Season" (*Expedition to Carthagena*, 147–48).

2. The British colony of the Leeward Islands extended from the Virgin Islands in the northwest to Dominica in the southeast.

Wednesday, 25 December 1751

Wednesday 25th

Christmas Day fine clear and pleasant with moderate Sea tho continuance of the Trade which by <o>bservation had set us in the Latitude of 18°.30'[1] We dined on <   > Irish goose which had be<en   > for the purpose some Weeks <Beef>[2] &ca &ca and drank a health to our absent friends.[3]

1. For other latitudes determined by observation, see the entry for 21 Oct., n.2.
2. For this word, see Toner, *Daily Journal*, 65, and Fitzpatrick, *Diaries*, 1:29.
3. GW's remarks on celebrating Christmas are the earliest known among his surviving papers.

Thursday, 26 December 1751

Thursday 26th

Clear with little or no Wind or Sea which want of Air to paliate the heat of the Sun made ~~it~~us truely sensible of ~~th~~its influence very permament and troublesome We had this Day for Dinner very fine Bristol Tripe with &ca.[1]

1. The ***Industry***, GW's ship, recently had arrived from Bristol, England (see p. 81 in the introductory essay to this part of the diary). Manufacturers in that city made special stoneware for this pickled delicacy, which generally comprised the lining of beef stomach. The Hamlin brand, imported into Barbados, became GW's favorite (see Walter, ***Memorials of Washington***, 43–44).

Friday, 27 December 1751

Friday 27th

Moderate Winds & Sea.

Saturday, 28 December 1751

Saturday 28th

Fresh gales from the NEt with squals of Rain & sudden change of the Air. Dined on a fine Irish Ling & Potatos.[1]

1. Barbados imported European salt fish, including the common ling, a long, cod-like fish plentiful in the waters around the British Isles (see Ligon, *True & Exact History*, 37, 39).

Sunday, 29 December 1751

<Sunday 29th>

Heavy Air with many Squals of Rain: the Wind wavering so that the Vessel often wou'd not lay her course.

Monday, 30 December 1751

Monday 30th

Clear Weather: & Wind from No. Et & Easterly blew very fresh.

Tuesday, 31 December 1751

Tuesday 31st

Thick and heavy with wavering Winds at 8 PM violent winds from the Westw<ard> with excessive Rain which got <to> the No. abt 12 and clear'd which being directly ahead & Mount<ai>nous [sea] running preventing carrying Sail but obligd < > to hinder the foresail < >.

Wednesday, 1 January 1752

Wednesday January 1<st>—1751[1]

The Wind still continuing at No. tho' not so violent we made Sail abt 12 and stood No.WBW saleing as near the Wind as we cou'd.

1. The year was 1752 according to the "New Style" calendar (see the discussion of "Dating the Entries" in the Editorial Methodology).

Thursday, 2 January 1752

Thursday 2d

The Sea greatly fallen & winded something aba<ted> tho still directly ahead which oblig'd us to keep the course we did the preceeding day.

Friday, 3 January 1752

Fryday 3

In the Morning Calm and clear; at noon the Wind breezed up at So. and clouded <over with> Rain and at 8 PM <became v>ery squally with some violent storms of Wind which before ten oclock got to No. Wt and remain'd there the Night with divers hard squalls of Wind & Rain.

Saturday, 4 January 1752

Saturday 4th

The Wind still at No. Wt directly ahead & Mountanous Sea we bore away NNE the whole day was attended with successive Squals.

Sunday, 5 January 1752

Sunday 5th

Wind continues at No. Wt tho much abated and clear Wea[ther] The Sea greatly fall<en > changed our course to <make an>other Tack.

Monday, 6 January 1752

Monday 6th

Last night the Wind varied to the So. ward and grew calm at 6 AM freshned and had got to West we made another tack and stood No. No. Wt this day Warm & pleasant.

Tuesday, 7 January 1752

Tuesday 7th

Wind fresh & Wavering with some Squals & rough Sea.

Wednesday, 8 January 1752

Wednesday 8th

~~L~~About 2 this morning the Wind died away and at < u>p[1] at No. Wt and variable <with some> hard Squals of Wind & Rain by Observation were in the Latitude of 32°.30' the Mared[ia]n of Bermudos.[2]

1. GW probably wrote a time and a phrase like "sprang up" here, where material has been lost through mutilation (see the entries for 20 and 29 Jan.).

2. This latitude is about ten nautical miles north of Bermuda. Apparently GW meant parallel when he wrote meridian.

Thursday, 9 January 1752

Thursday 9th

At 2 A:M came on excessive hard Wind at No. Wt; Rain Lightning & some thunder the Wind increased so violently & had raiz'd so Mountanous a Sea that oblig'd the handing all her Sails & driving with bear Masts which She did untill 4 P:M: when th<e> Wind had something ~~aba~~Moderated and Sea abated and then She was laid too under <the main> Stay Sail[1]—this day < > me a Criple by the Ships <rolling>.[2]

1. For GW's subsequent use of this phrase, see his entries for 12, 14, and 18 January.
2. GW undoubtedly alludes here to seasickness (see his entry for 23 Dec.).

Friday, 10 January 1752

Fryday 10th

This Morn<ing the> Wind was moderate tho di<rectly a>head about 8 A:M we made sail and stood W:S:W upon searching my chest discover'd I had been rob'd of 16 pistoles[1] at 2 P:M the Wind had changed to So. Wt and blew fresh which increasing obliged us to hand all but the fore Sail, and that cou'd be carryed no longer than 12 when the Wind was so Violent the Sea so high with great Quantity of Rai<n thu>nder & Sharp Light<ning > the Ship was Laid <to under a r>eefed fore Sail.

1. French and Spanish pistoles were gold coins customarily valued at 17s. 6d. each (see Edward Hatton, *The Merchant's Magazine: or, Trades Man's Treasury*, London, 1712, p. 128).

Saturday, 11 January 1752

<Satur>day 11th

The wind still as violent as ever (with many hard Squals of Rain) ~~th~~and got somewhat more to the Westward the Sea excessively high lay too all day.

Sunday, 12 January 1752

Sunday 12th

The Wind as violent as the preceding day with Rai<n> Hail & Snow & high & Mounta<i>nous Sea from WNWt Lay too all the Last night and this day under Main Stay Sail.

Monday, 13 January 1752

<Monday 13th>

This day < br (inferior[1] to> the former) <with> hard Wind high Sea Rain &<ca> &c. the Wind in the Same Quarter lay too [a]s[2] Yesterday.

1. This word and the letters "br" are from Toner, *Daily Journal*, 69, and Fitzpatrick, *Diaries*, 1:32. The lower portion of an open parenthesis is visible.
2. GW inadvertently wrote "is" here.

Tuesday, 14 January 1752

Tuesday 14th

Last night the Wind ceased of its violence & by 2 A:M was calm and continued so till 6 when it Sprung u<p> at East & came on Squals of Rain, much, & very Large hail with violent Thunder at 8 the Wind had got to the Wt of the No. and blew a fret[1] with cons<tant> Rain.

<A>s we carried S<ail w>hile it was at E<a>st < w>ere oblig'd to Lay too under <t>he Main stay Sail both by reason of the Winds being so excessive high & directly ahead before Night it was at No. Wt & there remain'd.

1. A "fret" can describe a gust or squall. As Daniel Defoe noted, "it was Happy for us that we had a stout Ship under us, for it blew a Fret of Wind" (*New Voyage Round the World*, 190).

Wednesday, 15 January 1752

Wednesday 15th

This morng the Wind was not so Violent as Yesterday but Still at No. Wt and so hard as to hinder us from carrying Sail the Day was squally with some Intermission of Sunshine which < >en sinc<e[1] an> observatio<n> was got and found ourselv<es> in the Latitude of 35<°>.00'.[2]

At 2 P:M: Espy'd a Sail laying too bearing So. Et abt a League dist[ant].

1. Mutilation obscures the top two lines of this page. The letters "en" and "sinc" appear in Toner, *Daily Journal*, 70, and Fitzpatrick, *Diaries*, 1:33.

2. Inclement conditions over the previous days likely prevented astronomical observations to verify the ship's latitude. For GW's most recent recorded reading, see the entry for 8 Jan.; see also the entry for 21 Oct., n.2.

Thursday, 16 January 1752

Thursday 16th

Moderate & clear with the Wind where it was made Sail & stood No. No. Et. abt 8 AM the Vessel we saw Yesterday came up and spoke with us She was from St Cits bound to Norfolk Matthew Stroud Com[mande]r. She was a Sloop calld the Glasgow had from us Candles Twine &c.[1] < >d promis< > upon comp< >[2] found them to agree nea<rl>y alike <a>nd that Cape Henry boar WNW abt 120 Leagues[3] She had been beating abt the Coast with contrary Wind 14 or 15 days with very rough Weather.

1. The 40-ton sloop *Glasgow* received bond at St. Kitts on 21 Nov. 1751. She had sailed from Port Hampton, Va., on 18 Oct. with a cargo of oats, pork, beef, corn, staves, shingles, and five boxes of candles. The vessel subsequently returned to St. Kitts and arrived at Port Hampton in late April 1752 with sugar, rum, and molasses (see P.R.O.: C.O. 5/1446, folios 52 [verso] and 54, Naval Office Shipping Lists for Virginia).

2. GW probably wrote something like "comparison of observations" here.

3. Assuming correct navigational reckonings, 360 nautical miles east-southeast of Cape Henry, Va., put the vessels in the vicinity of 35° N, 69° W.

Friday, 17 January 1752

Fryday 17th

Wind still at No. Wt. We had lost sight of the sloop and abt 6 AM discovered another Vessel which came up with us abt 10 She also was from St Christopher's a Billander[1] ~~& had~~bound to Philidelphia ~~She~~& had been out five Weeks: and ten days ago < > of Cape <Henry[2] > of Water < di>scover'd another Sai<l b>earing No. Wt abt 2 Leagues a<nd> standg close to Windward as She cou'd whether it was the Sloop we saw Yesterday or not it was too far to distinguish—this Philiadelphia Man proposed keeping Company and also of going into Virginia if he saw no better prospect the t~~o~~wo Captns mutually ag[reein]<g>[3] to alter their Course at 6 oclock & westward.

1. A bilander carried two masts with a trapezoidal mainsail. Dutch merchants typically used the vessel along coasts and canals.

2. Mutilation obscures the top 2½ lines of this page. Earlier editions support this reading (see Toner, *Daily Journal*, 71, and Fitzpatrick, *Diaries*, 1:34).

3. See Toner, *Daily Journal*, 72, and Fitzpatrick, *Diaries*, 1:34.

Saturday, 18 January 1752

<Sat>urday 1<8th>[1]

< cha>nged and g< cam>e[2] on very fresh with < The> other Ship was very Sociable in keeping company being seldom more than a ¼ Mile dist[ant] both steering West[3] as the day advanced the Wind increased with continued Rain and by 10 P:M was oblig'd to hand all our Sails and lay too under a Stay Sail reefd at 11 lost sight of the Vessel.

1. Mutilation at the top of this page obscures the dateline and the first lines of the entry.
2. GW most likely is describing gales of wind here.
3. For GW's ship joining a bilander, see the entry for 17 January.

Sunday, 19 January 1752

Sunday 19th

The wind had shifted from So. to No. and blew extreame hard with Mountainous Sea but moderating somewhat we < >.[1]

1. Mutilation to the upper half of the next page has taken away the last lines of this entry.

Monday, 20 January 1752

Mu<nday 20th>[1]

<The winds> died away; and < > this Morning wh< > time we had been out & <our pros>pect of arriving put the Capt<n up>on allowancing the Hands whi<ch> at 8 A:M was accordingly done at 10 the Wind sprang up So. Wt we made Sail and stood WNW—but before Midnight the Wind had got to West directly ahead blew excess<ive> hard with thunder & Lightning[2]

1. Mutilation obscures the dateline of this entry and portions of at least the first five lines.
2. Mutilation to the top of the next page makes it uncertain whether GW added remarks to this entry.

Tuesday, 21 January 1752

<Tuesday 21st>[1]

< >d N by < > was < >y with < > 10 P:M la<i>d the Ves<sel >.[2]

1. Mutilation to the top of the page has removed the dateline and all but fragmentary portions of this entry.
2. GW probably referenced wind at the start of this entry and the ship's course at its close.

Wednesday, 22 January 1752

<Wedn>esday 22d

The Wind had moderated and got to No. Wt. made Sail at 8 and stood WSWt and after alter'd as the Wind which by Noon had got to No. & we to WNW the skie quite clouded so that there was not the least appearance of S~~o~~un toward<s> night the Wind was fallen & in the Night grew calm.

Thursday, 23 January–Wednesday, 29 January 1752

< >[1] Since leaving < go>od observation wa<s> < l>atitude the agreeable <weather t>his day inticed the Mate to e<merge> from his Cabbin (as a snail w<ould be> enlivened by the genial heat of the Sun)[2] who since the third or four[th] day after leaving Barbados has been coob'd up with a fashionable disorder contracted there.[3]

< > at Noon abt < wi>nd ceased and wea<ther became bl>eak & clear.[4]

<Satur>day 25th[5]

The weathr extreame<ly> cold & clear with wind at No. Wt sounded at 8 AM with[ou]t bottom[6] stood SW by W by observation was in 37°.08' Latitude.[7]

< >n was go< >[8] < >d it seem'd g< an>d judged we were not < > the Number of birds; & <presence> of sedge & Marsh weed.[9] we s< > say and judg'd rightly for at 6 <P.M.> sounded in 22 Fathom Water the Wind breez'd up fair tho the Captn carried but small Sails for fear of getting too near Land before Morning.

< off> of Cap<e[10] brou>ght on a Calm < > out of the Capes.[11]

<Wednesday 29th>[12]

Early this Morning <the> Wind sprang up at So. Et. made <sa>il under easy Gales past the Cape[13] abt Sun's rising and got to the Mouth of York River abt 11 P:M and was met by a pilot boat[14]

1. Mutilation to the top of the next five pages complicates the precise dating of entries. The compromised condition of the manuscript calls for presentation of the surviving material in less exact form.

2. GW rarely used figurative language in this diary. For another example, see his personification of the ocean in the entry for 30 October. The snail metaphor suggests a close observation of

nature, while the phrase "the genial heat of the Sun" appears in a number of literary works from the period, including David Hume's *Three Essays, Moral and Political* (London, 1748), 24.

3. GW most likely is referring to venereal disease.

4. This text is on a separate page from material in the preceding paragraph.

5. If GW wrote "Sunday," he mistakenly recorded the date.

6. Sounding measured the depth of the water and also involved sampling the sea floor to determine proximity to land. To sound "without bottom" means the measuring device could not reach solid ground.

7. This position placed GW's ship at the mouth of Chesapeake Bay, probably close to Cape Charles, Virginia.

8. GW probably wrote "observation was got."

9. These sightings of birds and vegetation signaled proximity to shore.

10. For the previous three words, see also Toner, *Daily Journal*, 75, and Fitzpatrick, *Diaries*, 1:35.

11. This fragmentary text could be a continuation of the previous entry (although on a separate page) or part of a subsequent entry.

12. The *Industry* entered Port York, Va., on Thursday, 30 Jan. (see P.R.O.: C.O. 5/1444, folio 43, Naval Office Shipping Lists for Virginia). The ship's arrival supports the date for GW's diary entry.

13. GW presumably means Cape Charles.

14. GW disembarked from the vessel after a passage of over five weeks. The words "pilot boat" end at the page break; whether the entry continued onto the next mutilated page cannot be determined.

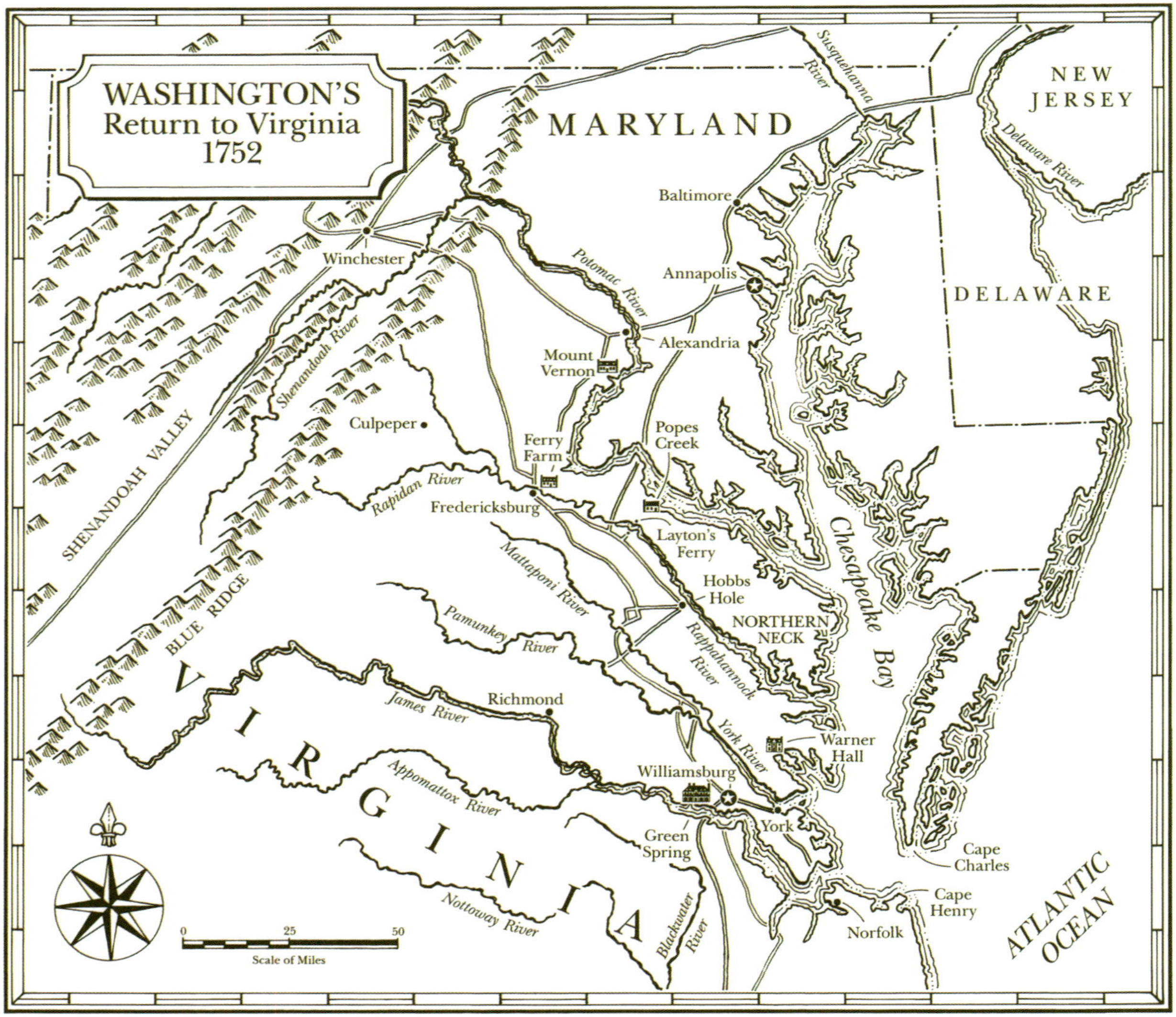

Washington's return to Virginia, 1752. (Illustrated by Rick Britton. Copyright Rick Britton 2017.)

BACK IN VIRGINIA

30 JANUARY–C.4 FEBRUARY 1752

George Washington set foot on land in southeastern Virginia on 30 Jan. 1752 after a harrowing five weeks at sea. His journey, however, still required a final stretch. Ferry Farm lay more than one hundred miles to the north,[1] and Lawrence's Mount Vernon was an additional forty miles distant. As the young man set out, carrying memories of his recent adventures on land and sea, he also looked ahead with both professional and romantic objectives.

Williamsburg

Washington first traveled to Williamsburg, where the colonial capital's population was still recovering from a smallpox epidemic that had killed 53 of the 763 known residents.[2] Nevertheless, it was a town on the rise, and the population easily exceeded 1,000 permanent and temporary residents during sessions of the General Assembly. At the time of Washington's visit, construction of a new meeting place for the assembly was well under way, to replace the original capitol building that had been destroyed by fire in 1747. The new structure would be completed in 1753.[3]

Wealthy residents built Georgian-style homes, and shops displayed a variety of goods. A clergyman who visited in 1759–60 credited the capital with about 200 private houses, as well as several public buildings, but asserted that Williamsburg "does not contain more than one thousand souls, whites and negroes; and is far from being a place of any consequence." He found more impressive "a handsome square in the center, through which runs the principal street, one of the most spacious in North-America, three quarters of a mile in length, and above a hundred feet wide."[4] This town square anchored the community. Local institutions included the College of William and Mary, with some seventy students and four professors, Bruton Parish Church, and a prison.[5]

Washington went to Williamsburg to deliver unidentified letters he was carrying from Barbados to Lt. Gov. Robert Dinwiddie (1692 or 1693–1770), whose London-based company owned a ship, *Jubilee*, that in 1751–52 exchanged rum, sugar, and slaves between Barbados and Virginia. Born in Scotland, Dinwiddie had become a trader and one of the richest men in Bermuda by the early 1720s. He initially entered government service when he was appointed British representative to Bermuda, and he eventually became surveyor-general of customs for the southern ports of America. That favorable post placed him in charge of customs for numerous British colonies in North America and the West Indies.[6]

King George II appointed Dinwiddie lieutenant governor of Virginia on 4 July 1751. As the colonial governor of Virginia resided in England, Dinwiddie carried out the duties of the colony's executive. Assembly members, including Lawrence Washington's father-in-law, William Fairfax, welcomed Dinwiddie upon his arrival in Williamsburg. The relationship between Dinwiddie and Fairfax dated to before 1739, and both men backed the Ohio Company, founded in 1747 as a land-speculation enterprise to encourage Virginians to settle the western frontier.[7] When Washington visited the lieutenant governor, it likely came as no surprise that Dinwiddie inquired about Lawrence's health. Lawrence's marriage to Ann Fairfax had given him access to Virginia's elite social circles, which included Dinwiddie. Washington no doubt was well aware of the social and professional advantages to be gained through connections to a man of Dinwiddie's status and power.

Professional and Military Aspirations

The last surviving entry in his diary records Washington's crossing of the Rappahannock, north of Williamsburg, on 4 Feb. 1752. By the end of that month, he had resumed surveying. He would complete at least thirteen professional surveys in the rest of that year.[8]

At the same time, he was exploring a military career. A letter George Washington wrote Dinwiddie on 10 June 1752 about adjutant general appointments likely echoes their conversation in Williamsburg. Lawrence Washington had been adjutant general for Virginia, but the position was to be divided among four newly created military districts: the Frontier, the Northern Neck and Eastern Shore, the Middle Neck, and the Southern District. In his letter, he discussed the intentions of William Fitzhugh (1721–1798), whose residency in Maryland complicated his desire to obtain a Virginia post. Washington emphasized his own interest in a position, promising to "take the greatest pleasure in punctually obeying from time, to time, your Honours commands; and by a strict observance of my Duty, render myself worthy of the trust reposed in Me."[9] His bid succeeded, and before the year ended he received a commission as major and adjutant of the militia, horse and foot, for the Southern District, which encompassed twelve counties.[10]

In 1753, Dinwiddie demonstrated his confidence in Washington when he sent him on a mission to meet the commander of the French forces in the Ohio Country and ascertain their intentions regarding land claimed by the British.[11] Washington completed his mission, but the French refused to vacate. Dinwiddie sent him back to the Ohio Country, having commissioned him a lieutenant colonel of Virginia troops in the resulting British campaign against the French. Not only did Washington's engagement with the French during this time give him his first taste of military combat, it also provided a catalyst for the conflict known as the French and Indian War.[12] He served under Dinwiddie until October 1754, when he resigned his commission as major in a Virginia militia regiment rather than accept a reduction in rank to captaincy in Dinwiddie's newly reorganized independent companies of the British army.

Design'd and Engrav'd by Will.m Hogarth

Pit Ticket

Publish'd according to Act of Parliament Nov. 5th 1759.

Entertainment and Romance

Before continuing north from Williamsburg, Washington went to York, where he attended a cockfight tournament—or "main"—which was a popular entertainment for all classes. Prizes of 5 pistoles were awarded for each contest, he reported, with a grand prize of 100 pistoles for winning the tournament.[13] He did not record whether he wagered any money on the proceedings. Following this diversion, he continued homeward.

Washington's first known letter after his return from Barbados was dated 20 May 1752 and sent to William Fauntleroy (1713–1793), whose daughter Elizabeth (1736–1792) had sparked his romantic interest. He apologized for his delay in visiting the Fauntleroys in Richmond County, but "Violent Pleurisie" had sickened him, and he needed to recover "strength to wait on Miss Betcy, in hopes of a revocation of the former, cruel sentence."[14] He enclosed a letter for the young woman and hoped for a change of heart. Alas, his second profession of love to Elizabeth was no more successful than the first, and she eventually married a man from Henrico County. He continued his quest for romance, and on 6 Jan. 1759 he wed the widow Martha Dandridge Custis.

---

1. The land across the Rappahannock River from Fredericksburg became known as Ferry Farm after GW's death.

2. See William Quentin Maxwell, ed., "A True State of the Smallpox in Williamsburg, February 22, 1748," *Virginia Magazine of History and Biography* 63 (1955): 269–74. Another estimate places the population of Williamsburg at 885 in 1748; see Cathy Hellier and Kevin Kelly, *A Population Profile of Williamsburg in 1748* (Williamsburg, Va., 1987), 2.

3. See Virginia Writers' Project, WPA, *Virginia: A Guide to the Old Dominion* (American Guide Series, New York, 1940), 321.

4. Andrew Burnaby, *Travels through the Middle Settlements in North-America, In the Years 1759 and 1760. With Observations upon the State of the Colonies* (London, 1775), 5–6. See also Burnaby to GW, 4 Jan. 1760 (*PGW-Colonial* 6:380–81).

5. See Osborne, *Williamsburg in Colonial Times*, and Goodwin, *College of William and Mary*.

6. For a full biography, see Louis Knott Koontz, *Robert Dinwiddie: his career in American Colonial Government and Westward Expansion* (Glendale, Calif., 1941); see also R. Alonzo Brock, ed., *The Official Records of Robert Dinwiddie, Lieutenant-Governor of the Colony of Virginia, 1751–1758* (2 vols.; Richmond, 1883–84).

Pit Ticket, or The Cock Fight (facing page), etching by William Hogarth, 1759. (Yale University Art Gallery, Gift of Mrs. William L. Harkness)

7. See Kenneth P. Bailey, *The Ohio Company of Virginia and the Westward Movement, 1748–1792: A Chapter in the History of the Colonial Frontier* (Glendale, Calif., 1939), and Alfred P. James, *The Ohio Company: Its Inner History* (Pittsburgh, 1959).

8. See *PGW-Colonial* 1:31.

9. *PGW-Colonial* 1:51.

10. See *PGW-Colonial* 1:53.

11. For more information on GW's journey to the French commandant, 31 Oct. 1753–16 Jan. 1754, see his journal of the expedition in *DGW* 1:118–61.

12. For GW's journal about his second Ohio expedition and resulting military engagement, 31 March–27 June 1754, see *DGW* 1:162–210. A thorough discussion of the war for empire can be found in Fred Anderson's *Crucible of War: The Seven Years' War and the Fate of Empire in British North America, 1754–1766* (New York, 2000). For GW's later reflections on his role in that war, see Fred Anderson, ed., *George Washington Remembers: Reflections on the French and Indian War* (Lanham, Md., 2004).

13. Arch Ruport, *The Art of Cockfighting: A Handbook for Beginners and Old Timers* (New York, 1949), 200.

14. *PGW-Colonial* 1:49.

THE DIARY ENTRIES

◆

Thursday, 30 January–Sunday, 2 February 1752

< >[1] Hired < to>[2] Williamsburg <with > Letters to the Gover<nor[3] who> had just gone to greenspring<s[4] for> Dinner as I got to the great <metro>polis; upon his return (whic<h was> at Night) I waited upon and wa<s> received Graciously he enquired kindly after the health of my Br[other] and invited me to stay and dine

< > things Lan< >

A Great Main of <coc>ks fought in Yorktown <bet>ween Gloucester & York for <5> pistoles[5] each battle & 100 the Odd[6] I left it with Colo. Lewis before it was decided & had part of his Chariot to his house[7]

< >s in M< >

1. Mutilation to the tops of the next four pages complicates precise dating of entries. The compromised condition of the manuscript calls for presentation of the surviving material in less exact form.

2. GW is referring to a mode of transportation, likely a horse or a carriage.

3. For more information on Governor Dinwiddie, see p. 104 in the introductory essay to this part of the diary. While GW presumably carried at least one letter of introduction, the letters he brought from Barbados have not been identified.

4. Philip Ludwell (1716–1767), a member of the governor's council, owned Green Spring plantation about five miles from Williamsburg.

5. The number follows Toner, *Daily Journal*, 76, and Fitzpatrick, *Diaries*, 1:36. For the gold coins called pistoles, see the entry for 10 Jan., n.1.

6. For more on cockfighting, see p. 107 in the introductory essay to this part of the diary. An odd number of battles removed the possibility of a tie.

7. John Lewis (1694–1754), father-in-law of GW's sister Betty, lived at Warner Hall in Gloucester County, approximately ten miles north of York.

Monday, 3 February 1752

Monday 3d

Fr<om >[1] his Chair[2] to M<ajr Dan >field[3]—at Hobs-Hole[4] who ~~kin~~<~~dly~~>.

1. For the last two letters of this word, see Toner, *Daily Journal*, 77, and Fitzpatrick, *Diaries*, 1:36.

2. Popular in the eighteenth century, riding chairs were more comfortable than horseback for both the rider and the horse. See Ed Crews, "Wheels and Riding Carts," *Colonial Williamsburg: The Journal of the Colonial Williamsburg Foundation* 27 (2005): 26–35.

3. The "M" is visible on the manuscript. "Majr Dan" is printed in Toner, *Daily Journal*, 77, and Fitzpatrick, *Diaries*, 1:36. See *DGW* 1:297 for the suggestion, without documentation, that GW visited Col. William Daingerfield (d. 1769) of Greenfield, Essex County.

4. Hobbs Hole (now Tappahannock) was a colonial trading post located about fifty miles northwest of Warner Hall.

Tuesday, 4 February 1752

Tuesday 4th

kindly convey<d> Me to Layton's Ferry where, I crossed[1] & was favoured with[2]

1. Layton's ferry crossed the Rappahannock River about twenty miles north of Hobbs Hole.
2. The page ends here. Only a few illegible words, pertaining to either this or a subsequent day, remain on the verso.

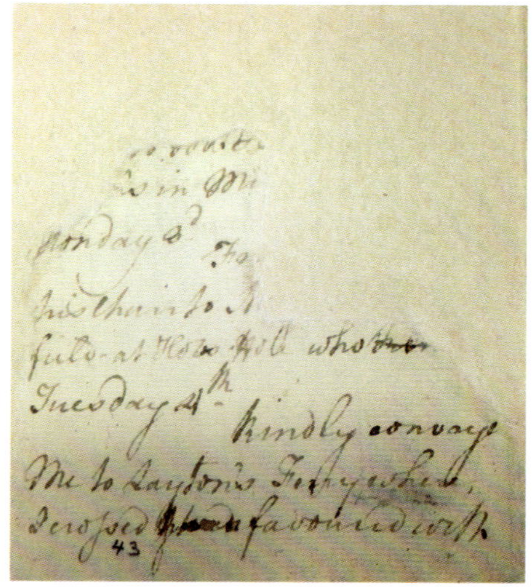

Entries for 2–4 Feb. 1752, George Washington, Diary, 1751–52. (George Washington Papers, Series 1, Exercise Books, Diaries, and Surveys 1745–99, Subseries 1B, Manuscript Division, Library of Congress; photograph by Alicia K. Anderson and Lynn A. Price)

APPENDICES

APPENDIX A
GLOSSARY OF NAUTICAL TERMS

Dictionaries and navigational texts used to compile the following definitions include James Atkinson's *Epitome of the Art of Navigation* (London, 1747) and *A Compleat System of Navigation* (Dublin, 1750); William Falconer, *An Universal Dictionary of the Marine...* (London, 1769); Darcy Lever, *The Young Sea Officer's Sheet Anchor, or a Key to the Leading of Rigging and to Practical Seamanship* (2nd ed., 1819; reprint, Mineola, N.Y., 1998); and the *Oxford English Dictionary*.

Diary dates, where they appear, indicate examples of a term's usage. Most words defined here appear in GW's ship's log or the account of his return voyage; the few that do not are included to provide necessary background information.

aft Behind the middle area of a ship; relating to the rear portion, or stern.

at From the direction of ("a Little breeze of Wind at WSW" is a breeze blowing from the west-southwest; 6 Oct. 1751 and throughout).

bare Having no sail up ("bare mast"; 9 Jan. 1752).

bear To head in a direction or toward a certain landmark. Also, to change course so the ship sails in a different direction (4, 28, and 29 Oct., 1 Nov., and 23 Dec. 1751; 15 Jan. 1752).

bearing The compass point of an object on the horizon (16–17 Jan. 1752).

bottom The seabed or sea floor. To sound "without bottom" is to fail to find the sea floor when testing for depth (23–29 Jan. 1752).

brig A vessel with two square-rigged masts, meaning sails set perpendicular to the ship's length and supported by horizontal beams called yards. Generally a merchant ship; often used interchangeably with "brigantine" (see p. 4 in the introductory essay to "Sailing to Barbados").

brigantine Most commonly, a brig with fore-and-aft rigging (meaning sails set parallel to the ship's length) on its mainmast (14 Oct. 1751).

buffeting The tossing and pounding of rough seas or winds against a vessel (30 Oct. 1751).

cabin A private room, often reserved for officers, aboard a vessel; sleeping quarters (23–29 Jan. 1752).

cape A point or extension of land projecting into the sea, as a peninsula (16–17 and 23–29 Jan. 1752).

captain The officer commanding a warship, or a courtesy title often given to the commander of a merchant vessel.

carry sail To have sails raised (31 Dec. 1751; 10, 14–15, and 23–29 Jan. 1752).

compass An instrument used to determine direction (19 Oct. 1751).

contrary winds Winds blowing from different directions or in opposition to the ship's course (25–27 Sept. and 25–26 Oct. 1751; 16 Jan. 1752).

course The direction or route traveled by a ship, or its projected path (throughout the text).

crowd sail To employ more sail in order to increase a ship's speed (17 Oct. 1751).

dead reckoning The practice of estimating a ship's position without the aid of celestial observation, by considering course, speed, and distance traveled, and allowing for drift and compass variation. Not as accurate as navigation by observing the sun or other celestial bodies (16 and 20 Oct. and 2 Nov. 1751). *See also* observation.

degree A unit of angular measurement equal to 1/360 of a circle (°). Latitude and longitude are expressed in degrees.

departure The distance in nautical miles due east or west of a given meridian or for a single day ("daily departure").

double-reef To tie back two portions of a sail in order to reduce its surface area in high winds (16 and 20–21 Oct. 1751). *See also* reef.

driving A ship's passive movement, as when it is carried at random by storm winds or an unruly current ("driving with bare masts"; 9 Jan. 1752).

embark To board a ship (22 Dec. 1751).

fallen Describes a diminished turbulence in sea or winds (2, 5, and 22 Jan. 1752).

fathom A unit of length or depth equivalent to six feet (23–29 Jan. 1752).

flying jib Typically, the outermost of four jib sails on a square-rigged vessel (12 Oct. 1751). *See also* brig; jib.

foresail The sail stretched upon the foremast, which is the mast in front of the mainmast (21 Oct. and 31 Dec. 1751; 10 Jan. 1752).

foretopsail The sail set upon the foretopmast, above the foresail (13, 16, and 21 Oct. 1751).

fresh winds Strong, but not violent, winds; when a gale increases, it is said to "freshen" (12, 15–16, 18, 23–24, and 28 Oct., and 24, 28, and 30 Dec. 1751; 6–7, 10, and 18 Jan. 1752).

gale A sustained strong wind, but with less force than a hurricane; a "hard gale" is more tempestuous (9, 12, 15, 17, 28–29, and 31 Oct., 24 and 28 Dec. 1751; 23–29 Jan. 1752).

hand One of the crew (22 Oct. 1751; 20 Jan. 1752). Also, to furl or roll a sail close to its mast, yard, or stay, and fasten it there (12 and 16 Oct. 1751; 9–10 and 18 Jan. 1752).

hurricane A violent tempest, generally preceded by a calm and characterized by powerful opposing winds, an agitated sea, and thunder and lightning. Common between the tropics, especially in the Atlantic, and most prevalent in the northern Atlantic from June through November (19 Oct. 1751).

jib A triangular staysail set before the foremast (3 Oct. 1751).

knot A unit of speed of a moving ship or wind current. One knot is equal to one nautical mile per hour. Derived from the knotted log-line used to take this measurement.

large sea A high, tumultuous sea (17–18 and 22 Oct., and 23 Dec. 1751).

latitude Distance north or south of the equator, delineated by imaginary lines that run parallel to the equator and perpendicular to meridians of longitude. Latitude lines, also called "parallels," are equivalent to the angular distance of the pole above the horizon, expressed in degrees and minutes (e.g., 14°39'; 1–2 Nov., 23 and 25 Dec. 1751; 8, 15, and 23–29 Jan. 1752; and throughout charts).

lay To sail in the desired direction ("lay her course"; 29 Dec. 1751; 21 Jan. 1752). Also, to hold a ship stationary through the counterposition of sails ("lay to"; 21 Oct. 1751; 9–15 and 18 Jan. 1752).

league A unit of distance equal to 3 nautical miles (4 Oct. and 2 Nov. 1751; 15–17 Jan. 1752).

leeward Being in or facing the direction toward which the wind blows. Going "to leeward" is going with the wind (2 Nov. 1751). Opposite of "windward."

log-line A line attached to a log as part of the apparatus used to determine a ship's speed.

longitude Distance east or west, delineated by imaginary lines that run perpendicular to the equator and intersect at the poles. Longitude lines, also called meridians, are equivalent to the angular distance east or west of a standard (or "prime") meridian, expressed in degrees and minutes (e.g., 52°33').

main foresail The principal sail extended on the foremast (21 Oct. 1751).

mainmast The principal mast on a sailing ship.

mainsail The principal sail extended on the mainmast (17 Jan. 1752, n.1).

main staysail The storm sail set on the mainstay, which is the rope that runs from the top of the mainmast to the foot of the foremast (12 and 14 Jan. 1752).

main topsail The sail set on the main topmast, above the mainsail (16 and 28 Oct. 1751).

make sail To spread a greater quantity of sail in order to increase a ship's speed (throughout).

mast A vertical wooden pole to which are attached the yards, sails, and rigging (17 Oct. 1751; 9 Jan. 1752).

mate In a merchant vessel, an officer who assists the captain or pilot with navigation and ship management (23–29 Jan. 1752).

meridian *See* longitude (8 Jan. 1752 and throughout the charts).

minute A unit of angular measurement equal to 1/60 degree ('; throughout the charts).

mountainous sea A sea with very large waves (31 Dec. 1751; 4, 9, 12, and 19 Jan. 1752).

mouth The place where a river or stream enters the sea or other large body of water (29 Jan. 1752).

nautical mile A unit of distance at sea, equivalent to 1.15 land miles or one minute of latitude.

observation Determining one's latitude by measuring the altitude of the noon sun or a star. Often used to correct position previously determined by dead reckoning (21–23 Oct., 25 Dec. 1751; 8, 15–16, 23–29 Jan. 1752).

octant An instrument used for observing altitudes of celestial bodies. *See also* latitude.

out The condition of sails when they are set,

or extended, for sailing (20 Jan. 1752).

pilot boat A vessel used near the coast to guide a ship into bays, rivers, or harbors (23–29 Jan. 1752).

plummet A metal weight, often lead, connected to a line and dropped overboard to measure depth. *See also* sounding.

reckoning *See* dead reckoning.

reef To tie back a portion of a sail in order to reduce its surface area in high winds (13, 16, and 20–21 Oct. 1751; 10 and 18 Jan. 1752). *See also* double-reef.

refit To repair, restore, or equip a vessel or its parts (22 Oct. 1751).

right To adjust or restore to its proper state or condition (5 Oct. 1751).

rigging The system of lines (ropes) that support a vessel's masts (5 and 22 Oct. 1751).

schooner A sailing vessel with two (occasionally three) masts rigged fore-and-aft; a schooner can carry one or more square-rigged foretopsails (5 Nov. 1751).

set (the sails) To unfurl and extend the sails of a ship, exposing them to the wind (28 Oct. 1751).

signal (flag) A flag or flags used by a ship to communicate with other ships (20 Oct. 1751).

sloop Typically, a small vessel with one mast rigged fore-and-aft (4, 20, and 28–30 Oct. 1751; 16–17 Jan. 1752).

sounding The practice of measuring water depth (in fathoms) using a sounding line and plummet (23–29 Jan. 1752).

spritsail A square sail extended by a yard under the bowsprit, which is the pole projecting from a ship's bow (12 Oct. 1751).

squall A sudden violent wind, often accompanied by precipitation (13, 16, 18–21, 25 Oct., 28–29 Dec. 1751; 3–4, 7–8, 11, 14–15 Jan. 1752).

stand To head in a direction or hold a course. Also, to be in a certain compass direction relative to the observer (14 Oct. 1751 and throughout).

staysail A triangular sail extended upon a stay, or supporting rope, between masts (2 Oct. 1751; 9 and 18 Jan. 1752).

stern The rear part of a ship (7 Oct. 1751).

swell Agitated surf running in a particular direction, or the fluctuating motion of waves after a storm (14 and 23 Oct., and 23 Dec. 1751).

tack To turn a vessel by means of its sails and rudder against the wind (24 Oct. 1751; 5–6 Jan. 1752).

trades (trade winds) Winds continually blowing between the north and east in the tropics of the northern Atlantic. Known for aiding navigation and commerce (30 Oct., 23 and 25 Dec. 1751).

unbend To cast loose the sails from their yards and stays (28 Oct. 1751).

under sail Describes an unanchored ship governed by her sails and rudder. Also, having the sails set (2 and 20 Oct. 1751; 9, 12, 14, and 18 Jan. 1752).

up Describes a course to windward (2 and 21 Oct. 1751).

variable winds Inconstant winds changing direction and intensity (13–14 Oct. 1751; 8 Jan. 1752).

veer To alter the direction of (19 Oct. 1751).

vessel A general name given to a ship; especially applied to a smaller ship with one or two masts (25–27 Sept. and 29 Dec. 1751; 16–18 Jan. 1752).

weigh anchor To hoist the anchor in preparation for sailing (22 Dec. 1751).

windward The direction from which the wind blows. To stand "close to windward" is to head nearly against the wind (2 Nov. 1751; 17 Jan. 1752). Opposite of "leeward."

yard A horizontal pole that supports a square sail. *See also* mast.

APPENDIX B
COMPREHENSIVE CHART OF NAVIGATIONAL DATA AND COMPUTATIONS

Due to mutilation of the manuscript, significant portions of the ship's log are either missing or unreadable. The chart in this appendix combines Washington's surviving recorded navigational data and editorial calculations to produce a table for all thirty-five known days of the voyage from Virginia to Barbados.

Background

Though myriad navigational manuals would have been available to the young George Washington, he most likely studied James Atkinson's *Epitome of the Art of Navigation*, which he could find in his half brother Lawrence's library (see p. 3 in the introductory essay to "Sailing to Barbados"). Atkinson believed that "keeping a good *Reckoning* or *Journal*" maintained "the *Mariner's* Reputation" and, with God's providence, preserved the ship. Atkinson denounced "Ignorance" in reckoning as "the chief Cause of losing divers Rich Ships, and many dear Lives, and thence the impoverishing of several Families."[1]

Washington's diligence and precision favored his record keeping. Atkinson detailed the necessary procedures, from choosing the right paper, to ruling it into the requisite grid, to noting the appropriate contents for entries: "Transactions" of the day, "as *Winds, Weather, Currents, setting of the Sea, handing of Sails, meeting or parting with Ships, Death of Men, Variation of the Compass*, and all other *Accidents* and *Occurrences* whatsoever."[2]

The prime meridian, the reference point for determining longitude, was standardized in 1884 as an imaginary line running north–south through the Royal Observatory in Greenwich, England. Earlier English logbooks used the meridian of either London or "the Lizard"—a peninsula in Cornwall that marks the southernmost point of the British mainland—as the longitude from which all others were measured.[3] The mariner then chose the nearest local meridian, known to be a certain number of degrees from the prime meridian, as the starting longitude. Washington followed the practice of his era and used Philadelphia, at about 75° west of London, as the starting point from which he measured the vessel's distance traveled to the east.[4]

The Chart

Following sea time, in which the day begins at noon, these figures represent cumulative data recorded at the end of each day from 28 Sept. to 1 Nov. 1751. A row of figures covers each day, and each row has eight columns. The same row of figures can be found along the bottom of the log entry for the corresponding date. The data entered for hours, knots, course, and winds found at the beginning of each table are reflected in the columns for average course and the day's distance traveled.

To compute the estimated distances traveled and resulting positions, the editors deployed plane trigonometry. Square brackets designate editorially supplied text. A description of each cell and its computation follows.

1. Departure

Column 1 represents the vessel's daily departure, or the distance traveled in nautical miles east or west of the starting longitude on that day. It is equivalent to the sine of the average course (column 2) multiplied by the distance (column 3). Eighteenth-century ships carried printed tables of the sines and cosines for every angle, expressed in degrees and minutes. The departure figure then allows calculation of the day's change in longitude (column 7).

2. Course

Column 2 reflects the vessel's daily course, or the ship's direction on a given day. It is the average of all the directions recorded in the course column in the main table. Each direction has a corresponding angular measurement from 0° to 90°, which is easily determined from Washington's "A Table of the Angles" (see p. 8 in the introductory essay to "Sailing to Barbados"). Error is prevalent in this computation because of magnetic compass deviation and miscalculation.

3. Distance

The estimated number of nautical miles traveled in a day appears in column 3. The calculation involves the sum in nautical miles of the ship's speed from the knots column in the main table multiplied by two to represent a twenty-four-hour period. In cases when the latitude was measured directly by "observation," the exact distance could be calculated by dividing the difference of latitude (column 4) by the cosine of the course (column 2). This number was then used to correct the estimated distance.

4. Difference of Latitude

Column 4 shows the daily distance traveled in degrees and minutes to the north or south of the initial latitude. Since degrees of latitude are spaced equally across the globe, the distance traveled north or south in nautical miles is the same as that traveled in minutes. In other words, one nautical mile is equivalent to one minute. Thus, the difference of latitude equals the cosine of the average course (column 2) multiplied by the day's distance (column 3). Though Washington occasionally labeled this column with minutes and seconds, his logbook shows no unit smaller than the minute. This number allows computation of the day's latitude (column 5) in relation to that of the previous day.

5. Latitude

This is the absolute northerly or southerly position of the vessel on the globe. It can be computed or directly measured. Calculation takes the previous day's latitude (column 5) plus or minus the current day's difference of latitude (column 4). "Observation" occurred on days when the sun was visible at noon and an octant measured the sun's altitude over the horizon. A chart of declinations then identified the latitude (see the entry for 21 Oct., n.2).

6. Meridian Distance

Column 6 represents the total departure, or the total distance in nautical miles traveled to the east or west of the local meridian (in Washington's case, Philadelphia). It is the cumulative sum of all the departures recorded in column 1 since the first travel day, added to the first recorded meridian distance. Note, however, that when a day's travel runs in the opposite direction of the general course, the recorded departure for that day implies a negative number (see, for instance, the westward departure for 1 Oct. 1751).

7. Difference of Longitude

Column 7 shows the daily distance traveled in degrees and minutes to the east or west of the starting longitude. Because the distance between meridians shrinks closer to the poles, each degree of longitude has a unique length in nautical miles at a given latitude. Mariner charts provided these ratios. To compute the difference of longitude, the day's departure (column 1) is divided by the ratio, which, manually calculated, is always equivalent to the cosine of the latitude (column 5). The difference of longitude then allows computation of the day's longitude (column 8) in relation to that of the previous day.

8. Longitude

This is the absolute easterly or westerly position of the vessel on the globe. In Washington's time, it could be figured only from the previous day's longitude (column 8) plus or minus the current day's difference of longitude (column 7).

Date	1. Departure (nm)	2. Course (average)	3. Distance (nm)	4. Difference of Latitude (°/')	5. Latitude, North (°/')	6. Meridian Distance (nm)	7. Difference of Longitude (°/')	8. Longitude, West (°/')
28 Sept. 1751					[35°43']	[170 E]		[70°55']
29 Sept. 1751	[49 E]	SEBS	89	74' [S]	34°29'	219 E	60' E	69°55'
30 Sept. 1751	[52 E] [5]			[27' S]	[34°02']	[271 E]	[64' E]	[68°51']
1 Oct. 1751	[23][6] W	SW¾W	36	28' S[7]	33°34'	[248 E]	28' [W]	69°19'
2 Oct. 1751	[35 E] [8]			[03' N]	[33°37']	[283 E]	[43' E]	[68°36']
3 Oct. 1751	[11]9 E	E	119	00°00'	33°37'	402 E	142' E	66°[14']
4 Oct. 1751	[58] E	E	58	00°00'	33°37'	460 [E]	70' E	65°[04']
5 Oct. 1751	[7]3 E	EBS	75	00°13' S	33°24'	533 E	87' E	63°37'
6 Oct. 1751	39 E	E½S	39	00°03' N[9]	33°27'	572 E	00°46' E	62°[51']
7 Oct. 1751	[4]6 E	E¼S	46[10]	00°02' S	33°25'	618 E	00°55' E	61°54' [11]
8 Oct. 1751	66 E	ESE	71	00°27' S	32°58'	684 E	01°19' E	60°[35']
9 Oct. 1751	[9]4 E	EBS¾S	100	00°31' S[12]	32°27'	778 E	01°50' E	58°45'
10 Oct. 1751	86 E	SEBE	105	00°57' [S]	31°30'	864 E	01°40' E	57°[05']
11 Oct. 1751	[5 E] [13]	SBE	27[14]	00°26' S	31°04'	870 E[15]	00°06' E	56°59'
12 Oct. 1751	79 [E]	EBS	81	00°14' N[16]	31°18'	949 E	01°32' E	5[5°27']
13 Oct. 1751	[5]9 [E]	E	59	00°00'	31°18'	1008 E	01°09' E	54°18'
14 Oct. 1751	[18] E	SEBE	22	00°12' S	31°06'	1026 [E]	00°21' E	[53°57']
15 Oct. 1751	19 W[17]	SBW	80	01°16' S[18]	29°50'	1007 E	00°22' W	54°19'
16 Oct. 1751	[75] W	WSW	80[19]	30' [S]	29°20' [20]	932 E	01°26' [W]	55°[45']
17 Oct. 1751	25 E	SE½E	33	00°21' [S]	28°59'	957 E	00°29' E	55°16'
18 Oct. 1751	[9] E	S½E	92	01°31' S	27°28'	966 E	00°10' E	[55°06']
19 Oct. 1751	[1]2 W	SSW	33	00°30' S	26°58'	954 E	00°14' W	55°20'

(continued)

Date	1. Departure (nm)	2. Course (average)	3. Distance (nm)	4. Difference of Latitude (°/')	5. Latitude, North (°/')	6. Meridian Distance (nm)	7. Difference of Longitude (°/')	8. Longitude, West (°/')
20 Oct. 1751	[3]7 E	EBN¾N	40	00°13' N	27°11'[21]	991 [E]	00°42' E	54°[38']
21 Oct. 1751	[29] E	NEBE	35[22]	00°19' [N]	27°30'[23]	1010 [E][24]	00°33' E	54°05'
22 Oct. 1751	8 E	SSE	21[25]	00°19' S	27°11'[26]	1018 E	00°09' E	5[3°56']
23 Oct. 1751	[1]2 W	SSW	32[27]	00°29' S	26°42'[28]	1006 E	00°14' [W][29]	54°10'
24 Oct. 1751	[35] W	SW½W	46[30]	00°29' [S]	26°13'	971 E	00°39' [W][31]	[54°49']
25 Oct. 1751	54 E	E¾S	55[32]	00°08' [S]	26°05'	1025 E	01°00' [E]	53°49'
26 Oct. 1751	[69 E]	ESE	75	00°29' S	25°36'	[1094] E	[01]°16' E	[51°05'][33]
27 Oct. 1751	[0]	S	28	00°28' S	25°08'	1094 E	00°00'	51°05'
28 Oct. 1751	[6 W][34]	[S]½W	132	02°12' [S]	22°5[6]'	[1088] E	[00°07' W]	[51°12']
29 Oct. 1751	5 W	S¼W	103	01°43' [S]	21°13'	1083 E	00°06' W	51°18'
30 Oct. 1751	[23 W][35]	SBW	128	01°57' S[36]	19°16'	[1060] E	[00°]24' W	[51°42']
31 Oct. 1751	[13] W[37]	SBW	130	02°07' S	17°09'	1047 E	00°[14' W]	[51°56']
1 Nov. 1751	[27 W]	[SB]W	13[9]	02°16' S	14°5[3]'	[1020] E	[00°28' W]	[52°24']

1. Atkinson, *Epitome of Navigation* (1736), 265–66.

2. Ibid., 267.

3. See A. R. T. Jonkers, "Parallel Meridians: Diffusion and change in early-modern oceanic reckoning," in *Noord-Zuid in Oostindisch perspectief*, ed. J. Parmentier (The Hague, 2005), 17–42.

4. See Evans, *Geographical Essays*, 1. Since London is only 8' to the west of Greenwich, GW's computations and modern coordinates are used interchangeably throughout the volume.

5. The departure is closer to 53 nautical miles, but this number corresponds better with GW's meridian distance by 3 October.

6. According to the course, the departure should be 29 nautical miles. The difference in longitude, however, suggests that GW wrote 23, a computation made using the wrong course (SW½S).

7. Using the given course, the difference in latitude should be 21' or 22'. As with the departure, however, this computation was made using the wrong course (SW½S).

8. The departure is closer to 36 nautical miles, but this number corresponds better with GW's meridian distance by 3 October.

9. Unless GW's figure was corrected by observation, the vessel sailed southward on this date, giving a latitude of 33°21'.

10. The ship speeds in the top portion of the day's table indicate a distance of 44 nautical miles.

11. This should be 61°56'.

12. The course and distance suggest a difference of latitude of 33' or 34'. GW may have rendered this number from an observed latitude.

13. An earlier editor rendered "5" (Toner, *Daily Journal*, 27). Although GW's total departure suggests 6 nautical miles, 5 is more accurate, being the equivalent of 6' of longitude at this particular latitude.

14. The ship speeds in the top portion of the day's table indicate a distance of 21 nautical miles.

15. A more precise figure is 869.

16. Unless GW's figure was corrected by observation, the vessel sailed to the south, giving a latitude of 30°50'.

17. Using the given course, the departure should be 15 or 16 nautical miles. This computation appears to have been made using the wrong course (SBW¼W).

18. Using the given course, the difference of latitude should be 78' or 79'. As with the departure, it appears that GW used the wrong course (SBW¼W).

19. The ship speeds in the top portion of the day's table indicate a distance of 83 nautical miles.

20. This latitude was calculated by dead reckoning.

21. This latitude was calculated by dead reckoning.

22. The ship speeds in the top portion of the day's table indicate a distance of 29 nautical miles.

23. This latitude was measured by observation.

24. According to the departure, the meridian distance should be 1,020 nautical miles. The 10-mile discrepancy would, of course, carry over into succeeding days.

25. The ship speeds in the top portion of the day's table indicate a distance of 29 nautical miles.

26. This latitude was measured by observation.

27. The ship speeds in the top portion of the day's table indicate a distance of 38 nautical miles.

28. This latitude was measured by observation.

29. Although GW erroneously gave the direction as east, the adjacent longitudinal computation is correct.

30. The ship speeds in the top portion of the day's table indicate a distance of 69 nautical miles.

31. GW again used the wrong direction but presumably calculated the resulting longitude correctly.

32. The ship speeds in the top portion of the day's table indicate a distance of 65 nautical miles.

33. The correct longitude is 52°33'.

34. According to the course, the departure should be 13 nautical miles. The difference in longitude, however, suggests that GW wrote 6, a computation made using the wrong course (S¼W).

35. The departure is closer to 25 nautical miles, but this number corresponds better with GW's difference of longitude.

36. The course and distance suggest a difference of latitude of 125' or 126'. GW may have rendered this number from an observed latitude.

37. According to the course, the departure should be 25 nautical miles. The proposed difference in longitude, however, suggests that GW wrote 13, a computation made using the wrong course (S½W).

APPENDIX C
LAWRENCE WASHINGTON'S LETTERS FROM BARBADOS AND BERMUDA

Portions of letters that Lawrence Washington wrote after he left Virginia for Barbados with his half brother George are known only from Sparks, *Writings*, 2:422–23. The contents of these letters supplement George's observations in his diary and warrant inclusion in this volume. Sparks provided no explanatory or contextual notes; this appendix renders the Sparks transcription, with numbered notes added for improved clarity and with headings and datelines introduced to distinguish each letter.

Lawrence Washington to Thomas Fairfax

[Barbados, November or December 1751][1]

This climate has not afforded the relief I expected from it, so that I have almost determined to try the Bermudas on my return, and, if it does not do, the dry air of Frederic.[2] This is the finest island of the West Indies, but I own no place can please me without a change of seasons. We soon tire of the same prospect. Our bodies are too much relaxed, and require a winter to brace them up. However, some of the country gentlemen look well, and live to a reasonable age. We have no kind of bodily diversions but dancing, which frequently produces yellow fever. I am obliged to ride out by the first dawn of the day, for by the time the sun is half an hour high, it is as hot as at any time of the day. The gentlemen are very polite and hospitable.

Lawrence Washington to a Friend

[BERMUDA, 6 APRIL 1752][3]

I have now got to my last refuge, where I must receive my final sentence, which at present Dr. Forbes will not pronounce.[4] He leaves me, however, I think, like a criminal condemned, though not without hopes of a reprieve. But this I am to obtain by meritoriously abstaining from flesh of every sort, all strong liquors, and by riding as much as I can bear through several parts of the island.[5] These are the only terms on which I am to hope for life. My doctor is an excellent guide for me to follow, who, by a perseverance in a milk diet, has restored his constitution from a most desperate state. These are hard terms, but what he further adds is still worse, that, let me receive what benefit I may from this climate, the next winter in Virginia will not only render it of no service, but will most certainly destroy me, the truth of which assertion I am too well convinced of, by coming here too soon; for though I was much mended and had lost some of the worst symptoms of my disorder, yet the air being very keen brought all on again in a worse degree than ever, and so they yet continue. As my endeavour to overcome this cruel disorder has already cost me much money and fatigue, I should unwillingly give over the pursuit whilst any just foundation for hope remains. Six weeks will determine me what to resolve on. Forbes advises the south of France, or else Barbadoes.[6]

1. Sparks indicated that this letter was written a "few weeks" after arrival in Barbados. The Washingtons landed on 2 Nov. 1751.
2. Thomas Fairfax then resided in Frederick County, Va., a mountainous area about 60 miles northwest of Mount Vernon.
3. Sparks supplied the place and date for this letter.
4. George Forbes (c.1705 or 1710–1778), a native of Scotland, earned a medical degree from

the University of Aberdeen in 1734. He subsequently settled in Bermuda, where he gained a reputation as an excellent doctor and became a prominent figure in the local government.

5. About 665 miles east of Cape Hatteras, N.C., Bermuda is shaped like a fishhook and measures some 21 square miles. Its somewhat hilly terrain reaches elevations over 200 feet. Tobacco cultivation and curing, once the driving force behind the island economy, was supplanted by a shift from land to sea as maritime commerce took prominence in the mid-1680s. St. George's, the island's only population center during the time of Lawrence Washington's stay, was established in 1612 and served from that time until 1815 as the capital of Bermuda. It is often described as the oldest continually inhabited English town in the New World.

6. Following this, Sparks summarized: "In the same letter he expressed a strong wish, that his wife would come to him, as he thought, in any event, that he should remain there at least a year. He proposed, that George should accompany her to Bermuda, but he did not insist on her undertaking this voyage, leaving it to the decision of herself and her friends." Sparks then reported that Lawrence Washington "soon wrote again,—'The unhappy state of health, which I labor under, makes me uncertain as to my return. If I grow worse, I shall hurry home to my grave; if better, I shall be induced to stay longer here to complete a cure.'" Ann Fairfax Washington remained in Virginia. Her husband returned to Mount Vernon and died there in July 1752.

APPENDIX D
EDITORIAL METHODOLOGY

Diary transcription is as literal as possible while still maintaining readability. The volume follows these editorial policies:

1. Capitalization, Punctuation, and Paragraphing. Capitalization follows the manuscript. If a sentence begins with a lowercase letter, it is not capitalized. Punctuation in prose is rendered as written except in cases of double punctuation, where the second mark (generally a second period or a dash) is dropped. In the ship's log, double periods between geographic coordinates are standardized to single, and leader dots are deleted, as is trailing punctuation for which no significance has been determined. Throughout the diary, if a paragraph is missing terminal punctuation, the appropriate mark is added silently, with the exception of a few instances where a diary entry is truncated by mutilation.

2. Abbreviations, Contractions, and Symbols. Abbreviations and contractions that appear in the original manuscript are retained and not expanded. Whether punctuated in the manuscript or not, an abbreviation (defined as a word lacking its terminal letters) receives a period, with the exception of directional abbreviations. "N" and "SE," for instance, are reproduced as they appear in the diary manuscript, without added periods. Where the letter "B" appears in the midst of a directional abbreviation, it stands for the word "by"; thus "SEBS" indicates "southeast by south."

A contraction (or word that includes the terminal letter but lacks an internal letter or letters) does not end in a period. If a period appears at the end of a contraction within a sentence, the period is silently dropped in the transcription. All superscript letters are brought down to the line. If a shortened word is unclear, missing letters are supplied in square brackets: "Gun P[owder] T[reason]" or "lat[itud]e." When times of day are indicated, A.M. and P.M. are capitalized and punctuated according to their appearance in the manuscript and are always rendered with no space between the letters. When an expand mark (usually a short horizontal bar above an abbreviated or contracted word) appears in the manuscript, the word is transcribed in full without comment.

Symbols such as the ampersand (&) and those indicating units of currency, like the pound (£) and shilling (/), are retained. (See more on currency below.) The Old English thorn (þ, but by Washington's day essentially indistinguishable from the letter Y) is transcribed throughout as "th." Ligatures, such as æ, are reproduced as they appear in the document. The symbol **F** in the manuscript is retained and indicates the nautical term "foretop," as in "foretopsail." Fractions written over either horizontal or diagonal bars are standardized: ½, ¾. The mathematical symbols for degrees (°) and minutes (') are rendered as written. A space intentionally left blank is represented as "[ ]." Oversize braces are reproduced as closely as possible.

3. Currency. Note that £1 in the mid-eighteenth century was equal in value to 20s., while 1s. consisted of 12p. A guinea, which previously had been equivalent to £1, by this time had a value of 21s.

4. Errors and Edits. Editorially supplied text is indicated in square brackets. Alternately or incorrectly spelled words are left unchanged unless unintelligible, in which case the corrected or clarified term appears in square brackets, and the change is noted in annotation. When Washington recorded the incorrect time of day or provided the wrong calendar date to go with the day of the week, the correct time or date is provided in square brackets and the change explained in annotation.

Where Washington edited his own words, deletions are indicated as having been stricken from the text. If a letter or letters are written over with new text, the original reading is crossed out, and the superimposed letters are transcribed immediately following the struck-out text. Insertions are silently added at the place of their appearance.

If an unpunctuated catalog or a run-on sentence causes confusion, then the appropriate punctuation is supplied within square brackets for clarity.

In the ship's log, Washington occasionally recorded an incorrect direction. Such errors are treated editorially on a case-by-case basis. When his mistake is simply an entry error and is not reflected in related data, the correct direction is provided in square brackets and the change noted in annotation. When the incorrect notation introduces error into the resulting calculations, it is left as is, with the correct reading noted in annotation.

5. Mutilated and Illegible Text. The Barbados diary is one of the most mutilated documents among George Washington's papers. The following guidelines have been adopted to render deteriorated or obscured content:

- If part of a missing letter is still visible, it is reproduced without comment.
- Angle brackets indicate places where text was lost due to mutilation of the manuscript or to other factors that rendered the text illegible. When text appears between angle brackets, it has been supplied from other sources, such as earlier printed editions of the diary, or when editors have some other basis to provide a reading.
- Endnotes specifically describe extensive mutilations ranging from multiple words or sentences to entire missing pages.

6. Printed Sources. For the entries for 3 and 4 Nov. 1751, a printed source is all that remains (Sparks, *Writings*, 2:424). The shift of copy text is noted through the use of angle brackets and in annotation. Elsewhere, words and phrases are borrowed from the Toner and Fitzpatrick editions when there is no legible alternative. In these few instances, the appropriated text is enclosed in angle brackets and indicated by an endnote.

7. Dating the Entries. Many of the datelines throughout the diary are incomplete or missing due to mutilation. Days of the week and calendar days are supplied where needed, based on dates of surrounding entries or other contextual clues. Misdated entries are corrected in square brackets and noted in annotation. A full title line comprising the complete, correct date is supplied at the beginning of each individual entry throughout.

The Barbados diary was written during the transition from "Old Style" to "New Style" calendar. The Calendar Act of 1750–51 had two specifications, that Britain and her colonies would: (1) follow neighboring nations by starting the year on 1 Jan. instead of 25 March; and (2) adopt the Gregorian calendar, which was introduced elsewhere as early as 1582 and which ran eleven days ahead of the centuries-old Julian calendar. Washington dated his diary entries according to the Julian calendar and set 1 Jan. in 1751, although the formally recognized year was 1752. It was not until September 1752, several months after his return from the island, that the official switch from the Julian to the Gregorian calendar occurred and, in the course of a day, the date advanced from 2 to 14 September.

BIBLIOGRAPHIC MATERIAL

ESSAY ON SOURCES

Although the diary that George Washington kept during his trip to Barbados is relatively short, proper editing has required extensive research. The editors especially delved into eighteenth-century sources that provide contemporary perspectives on the people and places. The full range of materials used to elucidate Washington's Barbados diary can be found in the notes to this volume. The purpose of this bibliographic essay is to identify broad categories of these sources and to highlight collections or items of particular significance.

Archival Sources

Archival items form the foundation of this publication. The Papers of George Washington at the Library of Congress, Washington, D.C., is the preeminent collection for this edition because it contains the manuscript of the Barbados diary, along with Washington's school exercise books and a financial record book known as "General Ledger A." These sources offer insights into Washington's youthful education and his later purchasing habits and tastes. (Following this essay is a list of abbreviations for commonly used sources, most of them editions or repositories of primary Washington materials.)

The editors devoted many hours to poring over microfilm of the Naval Office Shipping Lists for Virginia, 1678–1769, and the much less complete ones for the West Indies, 1678–1825, found in the Colonial Office subset of the British Public Records Office. This editorial effort yielded detailed information on ships mentioned in the Barbados diary. Other holdings in the Public Records Office resolved perplexing research problems.

The collections at Mount Vernon supplied a useful document: "An Inventory of the Estate of Lawrence Washington Esqr. deceased, as Apprais'd by us the Subscribers the 7th & 8th of March 1753." Administrative files at The Washington Papers editorial project at the University of Virginia—destined for permanent archiving at Mount Vernon—provided background information on how and why the original facsimile edition of the Barbados diary was published in 1976. Time spent at the Barbados Department of Archives and the Barbados Museum and Historical Society turned up materials useful for identifying individuals prominent in the island's history but not covered in standard biographical sources.

Printed Primary Sources

Jared Sparks, Joseph M. Toner, John C. Fitzpatrick, Donald Jackson, and Dorothy Twohig prepared earlier editions of the Barbados diary. For a full assessment of their endeavors, see the essay entitled "A History of Published Editions of the Barbados Diary" at the beginning of this volume.

Other documentary publications and printed primary sources have contributed to this edition. The editors relied most heavily on volumes of *The Papers of George Washington* (Charlottesville, Va.): *Diaries of George Washington* (6 vols., 1976–79); *Colonial Series* (10 vols., 1983–95); *Revolutionary War Series* (25 vols. to date, 1985–); *Confederation Series* (6 vols., 1992–97); *Presidential Series* (19 vols. to date, 1987–); and *Retirement Series* (4 vols., 1998–99). The first volume of *Diaries* presents two other journals that George Washington wrote while a young man: "A Journal of my Journey over the Mountains began Fryday the 11th. of March 1747/8" (pp. 6–23), and "Journey to the French Commandant 31 October 1753–16 January 1754" (pp. 118–61). Also useful was John F. Carlyle, ed., *The Personal and Family Correspondence of Col. John Carlyle of Alexandria, Virginia* (privately printed, 2011).

The editors located pertinent information in issues of two eighteenth-century newspapers: the *Maryland Gazette* (Annapolis) and the *Virginia Gazette* (Williamsburg). Cultural context was gleaned from selections of the *Barbados Gazette* dating from before Washington visited the island that are anthologized in Kevyn Alan Arthur, ed., *Caribbean Treasure: A Trove of 18th-Century Barbadian Poetry and Prose* (Leeds, England, 2008). An account of a volcanic eruption in the Caribbean Sea that nicely contextualized Washington's log entry for 19 Oct. 1751 came from the *Gentleman's Magazine* for February 1752. Appleton P. C. Griffin, comp., *A Catalogue of the Washington Collection in the Boston Athenæum* (Cambridge, Mass., 1897), whose unassuming title belies its usefulness, is a vital resource for information on Washington's books.

Barbados

The essential starting points for printed literature on Barbados before 1850 are Jerome S. Handler's two compilations: *A Guide to Source Materials for the Study of Barbados History, 1627–1834* (Carbondale, Ill., 1971), and *Supplement to A Guide to Source Materials for the Study of Barbados History, 1627–1834* (Providence, 1991). Among the discoveries made in these volumes, the editors have benefited most from Richard Ligon, *A True & Exact History Of the Island of Barbadoes. . . .* (1657; reprint, London, 1673); Griffith Hughes, *The Natural History of Barbados* (London, 1750); Robert Poole, *The Beneficent Bee: or, Traveller's Companion. . . .* (London, 1753); Richard Hall, *Acts, Passed in the Island of Barbados. From 1643 to 1762 . . .* (London, 1764); George Frere, *A Short History of Barbados, from Its First Discovery and Settlement to The Present Time* (new ed.; London, 1768); Robert H. Schomburgk, *The History of Barbados . . .* (London, 1848); and James H. Stark, *Stark's History and Guide to Barbados and the Caribbee Islands . . .* (Boston and Barbados, 1893). A literary work that proved helpful is Nathaniel Weekes, *Barbados: A Poem* (London, 1754).

Many recent secondary works have informed editorial discussion of Barbados. Notable are Patricia A. Molen, "Population and Social Patterns in Barbados in the Early Eighteenth Century," *WMQ*, 3rd ser., 28 (1971): 287–300; Jerome S. Handler, *The Unappropriated People: Freedmen in the Slave Society of Barbados* (Baltimore, 1974), and

"Freedmen and Slaves in the Barbados Militia," *Journal of Caribbean History* 19 (1984): 1–25; Jerome S. Handler and Frederick W. Lange, *Plantation Slavery in Barbados: An Archaeological and Historical Investigation* (Cambridge, Mass., 1978); Karl Watson, *The Civilised Island, Barbados: A Social History 1750–1816* (Barbados, 1979); Hilary McD. Beckles, *Black Rebellion in Barbados: The Struggle Against Slavery, 1627–1838* (Bridgetown, Barbados, 1984), and *A History of Barbados: From Amerindian Settlement to Caribbean Single Market* (Cambridge, England, 2006); Jack P. Greene, "Changing Identity in the British Caribbean: Barbados as a Case Study," in *Colonial Identity in the Atlantic World, 1500–1800*, ed. Nicholas Canny and Anthony Pagden, 213–66 (Princeton, 1987); Pedro L. V. Welch, *Slave Society in the City: Bridgetown, Barbados 1680–1834* (Kingston, Jamaica, 2003); and Michael Hartland, *A Concise & Illustrated Military History of Barbados, 1627–2007* (Barbados, 2007).

George Washington

George Washington is the subject of an immense and rich biographical and interpretive literature. Biographies that offer particularly valuable insights into his early life and trip to Barbados include Rupert Hughes, *George Washington: The Human Being & The Hero, 1732–1762* (New York, 1926); Douglas Southall Freeman, *George Washington: A Biography* (7 vols.; New York, 1948–57); James Thomas Flexner, *George Washington: The Forge of Experience (1732–1775)* (Boston, 1965); North Callahan, *George Washington: Soldier and Man* (New York, 1972); Ron Chernow, *Washington: A Life* (New York, 2010); and Robert Middlekauff, *Washington's Revolution: The Making of America's First Leader* (New York, 2015).

Specialized studies especially valuable to the editors were Walter H. Mazyck, *George Washington and the Negro* (Washington, D.C., 1932); Bernhard Knollenberg, *George Washington: The Virginia Period, 1732–1775* (Durham, N.C., 1964); Philander D. Chase, "A Stake in the West: George Washington as Backcountry Surveyor and Landholder," in *George Washington and the Virginia Backcountry*, ed. Warren R. Hofstra (Madison, Wis., 1998), 159–94; Jack D. Warren Jr., "The Childhood of George Washington," *Northern Neck of Virginia Historical Magazine* 49 (1999): 5785–809; William M. Ferraro,

"George Washington's Mind," in *A Companion to George Washington*, ed. Edward G. Lengel (Chichester, England, 2012), 542–57; Fred Anderson, "George Washington's Mentors," in *Sons of the Father: George Washington and His Protégés*, ed. Robert McDonald (Charlottesville, Va., 2013), 21–30; and Philip Levy, *Where the Cherry Tree Grew: The Story of Ferry Farm, George Washington's Boyhood Home* (New York, 2013), and *George Washington Written Upon the Land: Nature, Memory, Myth, & Landscape* (Morgantown, W.Va., 2015).

A few works have focused specifically on Washington during his visit to Barbados: E. M. Shilstone, "The Washingtons and Their Doctors in Barbados," *Journal of the Barbados Museum and Historical Society* 20 (1953): 71–80; G. A. Wessel and S. Leacock, *Barbados and George Washington* (Barbados, 1958); Richard B. Goddard, comp., *George Washington's Visit to Barbados, 1751* (Barbados, 1997); and Jack D. Warren Jr., *George Washington's Journey to Barbados* (St. Michael, Barbados, 2001). The editors have found these treatments particularly valuable.

Seafaring and Navigation

The literature on seafaring and navigation stretches back centuries. Indispensable to the editors were the 1736 and 1747 editions of James Atkinson, *Epitome of the Art of Navigation*, as well as an enlarged version entitled *A Compleat System of Navigation* (Dublin, 1750). Standing out among useful older works were Daniel Defoe, *The Storm: or, a Collection Of the most Remarkable Casualties and Disasters Which happen'd in the Late Dreadful Tempest, both by Sea and Land* (London, 1704), and *A New Voyage Round the World . . .* (London, 1725); John Seller, *Practical Navigation . . .* (London, 1711); Guillaume François Antoine de L'Hospital, *An Analytick Treatise of Conick Sections . . .* (London, 1723); John Hadley, "The Description of a new Instrument for taking Angles," *Philosophical Transactions of the Royal Society* 37 (1731–32): 147–356; George Anson, *A Voyage Round the World, In the Years MDCCXL, I, II, III, IV. . . . Compiled From his Papers and Materials, By Richard Walter. . . .* (6th ed.; London, 1749); William Falconer, *An Universal Dictionary of the Marine . . .* (London, 1769); John Hamilton Moore, *The New Practical Navigator . . .* (London, 1793); David Steel, *The Elements and Practice of Rigging and Seamanship* (2 vols.; London, 1794); Thomas Truxtun, *Remarks, Instructions, and Examples relating to the Latitude & Longitude . . .* (Philadelphia, 1794); Ralph Walker, *A Treatise on Magnetism, with a Description and Explanation of a Meridional and Azimuth Compass . . .* (London, 1794); and Darcy Lever, *The Young Sea Officer's Sheet Anchor, or a Key to the Leading of Rigging and to Practical Seamanship* (2nd ed., 1819; reprint, Mineola, N.Y., 1998).

A robust secondary literature addresses the experience of sailing during the eighteenth century. Items consulted include *A Naval Encyclopedia: Comprising A Dictionary of Nautical Words and Phrases; Biographical Notices, and Records of Naval Officers; Special Articles on Naval Art and Science . . .* (Philadelphia, 1881); Marcus Rediker, *Between the Devil and the Deep Blue Sea: Merchant Seamen, Pirates, and the Anglo-American Maritime World, 1700–1750* (Cambridge, England, 1987); Philip Edwards, *The story of the voyage: Sea-narratives in eighteenth-century England* (Cambridge, England, 1994); Dava Sobel, *Longitude: The True Story of a Lone Genius Who Solved the Greatest Scientific Problem of His Time* (New York, 1995); Peter Earle, *Sailors: English Merchant Seamen, 1650–1775* (London, 1998); Michael Chenoweth, "The 18th Century Climate of Jamaica, Derived from the Journals of Thomas Thistlewood, 1750–1786," *Transactions of the American Philosophical Society* 93, no. 2 (2003): i–153; and Paul A. Gilje, *To Swear Like A Sailor: Maritime Culture in America, 1750–1850* (New York, 2016).

Caribbean and Atlantic World

A substantive and growing literature has explored virtually all corners of the Caribbean and greater Atlantic world over the past few decades. A sample of the titles that proved helpful with this edition includes April Lee Hatfield, *Atlantic Virginia: Intercolonial Relations in the Seventeenth Century* (Philadelphia, 2004); Richard S. Dunn, *Sugar and Slaves: The Rise of the Planter Class in the English West Indies, 1624–1713* (Chapel Hill, N.C., 1972); Arthur L. Stinchcombe, *Sugar Island Slavery in the Age of Enlightenment: The Political Economy of the Caribbean World* (Princeton, N.J., 1995); John J. McCusker and Kenneth Morgan, eds., *The Early Modern Atlantic Economy* (Cambridge, England, 2000); Andrew Jackson O'Shaughnessy, *An Empire Divided: The American Revolution and the British Caribbean* (Philadelphia, 2000); Elizabeth Mancke and Carole Shammas, eds.,

The Creation of the British Atlantic World (Baltimore, 2005); Jack P. Greene and Philip D. Morgan, eds., *Atlantic History: A Critical Appraisal* (Oxford, 2009); Matthew Mulcahy, *Hubs of Empire: The Southeastern Lowcountry and British Caribbean* (Baltimore, 2014); Mary Shayne Draper, "The Tropical Metropolis: Cities and Society in the Early Modern British Caribbean," PhD diss. (University of Virginia, 2016); and Jay Coughtry, *The Notorious Triangle: Rhode Island and the African Slave Trade, 1700–1807* (Philadelphia, 1981).

Works centered on religion that proved useful include Richard L. Kagan and Philip D. Morgan, eds., *Atlantic Diasporas: Jews, Conversos, and Crypto-Jews in the Age of Mercantilism, 1500–1800* (Baltimore, 2009); Carla Gardina Pestana, *Protestant Empire: Religion and the Making of the British Atlantic World* (Philadelphia, 2009); and Travis Glasson, *Mastering Christianity: Missionary Anglicanism and Slavery in the Atlantic World* (Oxford, 2012).

Virginia

Although Washington recorded only a few diary entries while in Virginia, his home colony looms large in this edition. Sources on Virginia governmental, economic, social, and demographic history that assisted the editors include Andrew Burnaby, *Travels through the Middle Settlements in North-America, In the Years 1759 and 1760. With Observations upon the State of the Colonies* (London, 1775); R. Alonzo Brock, ed., *The Official Records of Robert Dinwiddie, Lieutenant-Governor of the Colony of Virginia, 1751–1758* (2 vols.; Richmond, 1883–84); J. A. Osborne, *Williamsburg in Colonial Times . . .* (Richmond, 1935); Kenneth P. Bailey, *The Ohio Company of Virginia and the Westward Movement, 1748–1792: A Chapter in the History of the Colonial Frontier* (Glendale, Calif., 1939); Virginia Writers' Project, WPA, *Virginia: A Guide to the Old Dominion* (New York, 1940); Alfred P. James, *The Ohio Company: Its Inner History* (Pittsburgh, 1959); Mary R. M. Goodwin, *The College of William and Mary* (Williamsburg, Va., 1967); Donald M. Sweig, "The Importation of African Slaves to the Potomac River, 1732–1772," *WMQ*, 3rd ser., 42 (1985): 507–24; and Cathy Hellier and Kevin Kelly, *A Population Profile of Williamsburg in 1748* (Williamsburg, Va., 1987).

Medical

The Washington brothers sailed to Barbados because of Lawrence's pulmonary disorder, and young George contracted smallpox after they arrived. The prevalence of sickness in the Barbados diary prompted the editors to consult a number of medical texts and studies. Most helpful were William Hillary, *A Rational and Mechanical Essay on the Small-Pox. . . .* (London, 1735); George Henry Fox et al., *A Practical Treatise on Smallpox, Illustrated by Colored Photographs from Life* (Philadelphia and London, 1902); Wyndham B. Blanton, *Medicine in Virginia in the Eighteenth Century* (Richmond, 1931); William Quentin Maxwell, ed., "A True State of the Smallpox in Williamsburg, February 22, 1748," *Virginia Magazine of History and Biography* 63 (1955): 269–74; C. C. Booth, "William Hillary—A Pupil of Boerhaave," *Medical History* 7 (1963): 297–316; Sheldon Watts, *Epidemics and History: Disease, Power and Imperialism* (New Haven, Conn., 1997); and Elizabeth A. Fenn, *Pox Americana: The Great Smallpox Epidemic of 1775–82* (New York, 2001).

Biographical

Sources for biographical information that have been used without citation include standard reference works such as *Dictionary of American Biography*, 20 vols. (New York, 1928–36); church and family records available through the Department of Archives in Barbados; and previous volumes of *The Papers of George Washington*. A select number of other biographical assessments offered background on important figures in the Barbados diary. These works include Edward D. Neill, *The Fairfaxes of England and America in the Seventeenth and Eighteenth Centuries . . .* (Albany, 1868); Louis Knott Koontz, *Robert Dinwiddie: his career in American Colonial Government and Westward Expansion* (Glendale, Calif., 1941); Peter R. Henriques, "Major Lawrence Washington Versus the Reverend Charles Green: A Case Study of the Squire and the Parson," *Virginia Magazine of History and Biography* 100 (1992): 233–64; and S. D. Smith, "Gedney Clarke of Salem and Barbados: Transatlantic Super-Merchant," *New England Quarterly* 76 (2003): 499–549.

Other Topics

Discussions of slavery, sugar cultivation, religion, women, leisure pursuits, and the environment appear in many of the works already mentioned in this bibliographic essay. Other titles have provided useful perspectives or information on these subjects and others. Notable are Arch Ruport, *The Art of Cockfighting: A Handbook for Beginners and Old Timers* (New York, 1949); Frank J. Klingberg, ed., *Codrington Chronicle: An Experiment in Anglican Altruism on a Barbados Plantation, 1710–1834* (Berkeley, Calif., 1949); J. Harry Bennett Jr., *Bondsmen and Bishops: Slavery and Apprenticeship on the Codrington Plantations of Barbados, 1710–1838* (Berkeley, Calif., 1958); J. Kumamoto et al., "Mystery of the Forbidden Fruit: Historical Epilogue on the Origin of the Grapefruit, *Citrus paradisi* (Rutaceae)," *Economic Botany* 41 (1987): 97–107; Hilary McD. Beckles, *Natural Rebels: A Social History of Enslaved Black Women in Barbados* (New Brunswick, N.J., 1989); and Larry Dale Gragg, *The Quaker Community on Barbados: Challenging the Culture of the Planter Class* (Columbia, Mo., 2009).

Also worthy of mention are Edward Littleton, *The Groans of the Plantations: or A True Account of Their Grievous and Extreme Sufferings By the Heavy Impositions upon Sugar, And other Hardships. Relating more particularly to the Island of Barbados* (London, 1689); William Cleland, *The Present State of the Sugar Plantations Consider'd; But more especially That of the Island of Barbadoes* (London, 1713); Richard B. Sheridan, *Sugar and Slavery: An Economic History of the British West Indies, 1623–1775* (Baltimore, 1973), and *Doctors and Slaves: A medical and demographic history of slavery in the British West Indies, 1680–1834* (Cambridge, England, 1985); Kathleen Wilson, *The Island Race: Englishness, empire and gender in the eighteenth century* (London, 2003); Russell R. Menard, *Sweet Negotiations: Sugar, Slavery, and Plantation Agriculture in Early Barbados* (Charlottesville, Va., 2006); Michael Craton, *Testing the Chains: Resistance to Slavery in the British West Indies* (Ithaca, N.Y., 2009); and Simon P. Newman, *A New World of Labor: The Development of Plantation Slavery in the British Atlantic* (Philadelphia, 2013).

ABBREVIATIONS

C.O. — Colonial Office (designating the location of documents in the Public Record Office).

DGW — Donald Jackson and Dorothy Twohig, eds. *The Diaries of George Washington*. 6 vols. Charlottesville, Va., 1976–79.

DGW-Abridged — Dorothy Twohig, ed. *George Washington's Diaries: An Abridgment*. Charlottesville, Va., 1999.

LC-Copy Book 1 — Library of Congress, George Washington Papers, Series 1, Exercise Books, Diaries, and Surveys 1745–99, Subseries 1A, Exercise Books 1745 to 1747: School Copy Book, Volume 1, 1745. https://www.loc.gov/item/mgw1a.002/. DLC:GW. Originally designated as Volume 2; see also *LC-Index*, xvii, xxvii.

LC-Copy Book 2 — Library of Congress, George Washington Papers, Series 1, Exercise Books, Diaries, and Surveys 1745–99, Subseries 1A, Exercise Books 1745 to 1747: School Copy Book, Volume 2, 1745. https://

www.loc.gov/item/mgw1a.003/. DLC:GW. Originally designated as Volume 3; see also *LC-Index*, xvii, xxvii.

LC-Index	Library of Congress, *Index to the George Washington Papers*, Washington, D.C., 1964.
LC-Ledger A	Library of Congress, George Washington Papers, Series 5, Financial Papers: General Ledger A, 1750–1772.
MVHR	*Mississippi Valley Historical Review,* 50 vols., 1914–64.
PGW-Colonial	W. W. Abbot et al., eds. *The Papers of George Washington, Colonial Series.* 10 vols. Charlottesville, Va., 1983–95.
PGW-Confederation	W. W. Abbot et al., eds. *The Papers of George Washington, Confederation Series.* 6 vols. Charlottesville, Va., 1992–97.
PGW-Presidential	W. W. Abbot et al., eds. *The Papers of George Washington, Presidential Series.* 19 vols. to date. Charlottesville, Va., 1987–.
PGW-Retirement	W. W. Abbot et al., eds. *The Papers of George Washington, Retirement Series.* 4 vols. Charlottesville, Va., 1998–99.

PGW-Revolutionary	W. W. Abbot et al., eds. *The Papers of George Washington, Revolutionary War Series.* 25 vols. to date. Charlottesville, Va., 1985–.
P.R.O.	Public Record Office, Kew, Surrey, England.
Vi	Library of Virginia, Richmond.
ViMtvL	Mount Vernon Ladies' Association of the Union, Mount Vernon, Va.
ViU	University of Virginia, Charlottesville.
WMQ	*The William and Mary Quarterly: A Magazine of Early American History*, Williamsburg, Va.

REFERENCES CITED

AMBLER, CHARLES H. *George Washington and the West.* Chapel Hill, N.C., 1936.

ANDERSON, FRED. "George Washington's Mentors." In *Sons of the Father: George Washington and His Protégés*, ed. Robert M. S. McDonald, 21–30. Charlottesville, Va., 2013.

ANDRIST, RALPH K., ed. *The Founding Fathers: George Washington, A Biography in His Own Words.* New York, 1972.

ANSON, GEORGE. *A Voyage Round the World, In the Years MDCCXL, I, II, III, IV.... Compiled From his Papers and Materials, By Richard Walter, M.A. Chaplain of His Majesty's Ship the Centurion....* 6th ed. London, 1749.

ARTHUR, KEVYN ALAN, ed. *Caribbean Treasure: A Trove of 18th-Century Barbadian Poetry and Prose.* Vol. 1. Leeds, England, 2008.

ATKINSON, JAMES. *A Compleat System of Navigation: In Two Parts. I. Atkinson's Epitome. II. Navigation New Modell'd....* Dublin, 1750.

———. *Epitome of the Art of Navigation; or, a Short and Easy Methodical Way to become a Compleat Navigator. Containing, Practical Geometry, ... Trigonometry,*

. . . with its Uses in Navigation, . . . The Description and Use of the Plain-Chart, Mercator's-Chart, both Globes, Hemispheres, and divers other Instruments. A New Form of keeping a Sea-Reckoning, or Account of a Ship's Way. . . . London, 1736; later edition, 1747.

Bennett, J. Harry, Jr. *Bondsmen and Bishops: Slavery and Apprenticeship on the Codrington Plantations of Barbados, 1710–1838.* Berkeley, Calif., 1958.

Callahan, North. *George Washington: Soldier and Man.* New York, 1972.

Carey, Mark. "Inventing Caribbean Climates: How Science, Medicine, and Tourism Changed Tropical Weather from Deadly to Healthy." *Osiris* 26 (2011): 129–41.

Chase, Philander D. "A Stake in the West: George Washington as Backcountry Surveyor and Landholder." In *George Washington and the Virginia Backcountry*, ed. Warren R. Hofstra, 159–94. Madison, Wis., 1998.

Chenoweth, Michael. "The 18th Century Climate of Jamaica, Derived from the Journals of Thomas Thistlewood, 1750–1786." *Transactions of the American Philosophical Society* 93, no. 2 (2003): i–153.

Chernow, Ron. *Washington: A Life.* New York, 2010.

[Cowley, J.]. *A Description of the Windward Passage, and Gulf of Florida, ... Also An Account of the Trade-Winds, and of the variable Winds and Currents on the Coasts thereabouts, at different Seasons of the Year. . . .* London, 1739.

[Defoe, Daniel]. *A New Voyage Round the World, by a Course never sailed before. Being a Voyage undertaken by some Merchants, who afterwards proposed the Setting up an East-India Company in Flanders.* London, 1725.

———. *The Life and Strange Surprizing Adventures of Robinson Crusoe, of York, Mariner: Who lived Eight and Twenty Years, all alone in an un-inhabited Island on the Coast of America, near the Mouth of the Great River of Oroonoque; Having been cast on Shore by Shipwreck, wherein all the Men perished but himself: With An*

Account how he was at last as strangely deliver'd by Pyrates. Written by Himself. 4th ed. London, 1719.

———. *The Storm: or, a Collection Of the most Remarkable Casualties and Disasters Which happen'd in the Late Dreadful Tempest, both by Sea and Land.* London, 1704.

———. *A Tour Thro' the Whole Island of Great Britain. . . . Giving A Particular and Entertaining Account of whatever is Curious and worth Observation . . . . Particularly fitted for the Perusal of such as desire to Travel over the Island.* 4 vols. 4th ed. London, 1748.

Draper, Mary Shayne. "The Tropical Metropolis: Cities and Society in the Early Modern British Caribbean." PhD diss., University of Virginia, 2016.

Dunn, Richard S. *Sugar and Slaves: The Rise of the Planter Class in the English West Indies, 1624–1713.* Chapel Hill, N.C., 1972.

Evans, Lewis. *Geographical, Historical, Political, Philosophical and Mechanical Essays. . . . Containing an Analysis Of a General Map of the Middle British Colonies in America . . . and the Maritime and Inland Navigations of the several Rivers and Lakes contained therein.* Philadelphia, 1755.

Faÿ, Bernard. *George Washington: Republican Aristocrat.* Boston and New York, 1931.

Fenn, Elizabeth A. *Pox Americana: The Great Smallpox Epidemic of 1775–82.* New York, 2001.

Ferraro, William M. "George Washington's Mind." In *A Companion to George Washington*, ed. Edward G. Lengel, 542–57. Chichester, England, 2012.

Fitzpatrick, John C., ed. *The Diaries of George Washington, 1748–1799.* 4 vols. Boston and New York, 1925.

———. *The Writings of George Washington from the Original Manuscript Sources, 1745–1799.* 39 vols. Washington, D.C., 1931–44.

Flexner, James Thomas. *George Washington: The Forge of Experience (1732–1775)*. Boston, 1965.

Fox, George Henry, S. D. Hubbard, S. Pollitzer, and J. H. Huddleston. *A Practical Treatise on Smallpox, Illustrated by Colored Photographs from Life*. Part 1. Philadelphia and London, 1902.

Freeman, Douglas Southall. *George Washington: A Biography*. 7 vols. New York, 1948–57.

Gilje, Paul A. *To Swear Like a Sailor: Maritime Culture in America, 1750–1850*. New York, 2016.

Goodwin, Mary R. M. *The College of William and Mary*. Williamsburg, Va., 1967.

Griffin, Appleton P. C., comp. *A Catalogue of the Washington Collection in the Boston Athenæum*. Cambridge, Mass., 1897.

Guthrie, William. *A New System of Modern Geography: or, A Geographical, Historical, and Commercial Grammar; and Present State of the Several Nations of the World. . . .* 2 vols. Philadelphia, 1794–95.

Hadley, John. "The Description of a new Instrument for taking Angles." *Philosophical Transactions of the Royal Society* 37 (1731–32): 147–356.

Hall, Richard. *Acts, Passed in the Island of Barbados. From 1643, to 1762, inclusive; Carefully revised, innumerable Errors corrected; and the Whole compared and examined, with the original ACTS, In the Secretary's Office. . . . And since his Death, continued by his Son, Richard Hall . . . .* London, 1764.

Handler, Jerome S. "Custom and law: The status of enslaved Africans in seventeenth-century Barbados." *Slavery and Abolition* 37 (2016): 1–23.

Hatfield, April Lee. *Atlantic Virginia: Intercolonial Relations in the Seventeenth Century*. Philadelphia, 2004.

Henriques, Peter R. "Major Lawrence Washington Versus the Reverend Charles Green: A Case Study of the Squire and the Parson." *Virginia Magazine of History and Biography* 100 (1992): 233–64.

Hillary, William. *A Rational and Mechanical Essay on the Small-Pox. Wherein The Cause, Nature, and Diathesis of that Disease, it's Symptoms, their Causes, and manner of Production, are explained and accounted for, according to the Laws of Motion, and Circulation of the Animal Fluids: With The Diagnostic and Prognostic Symptoms, through all the Stations of the Disease; and a new Method of treating it, so as to prevent the dangerous Symptoms, and fatal Consequences, which usually attend it. . . .* London, 1735.

Hughes, Griffith. *The Natural History of Barbados.* London, 1750.

Hughes, Rupert. *George Washington: The Human Being & The Hero, 1732–1762.* New York, 1926.

Keagy, Thomas J. "The Poor Whites of Barbados." *Revista de Historia de América* 73/74 (1972): 9–52.

Klingberg, Frank J. Introduction to *Codrington Chronicle: An Experiment in Anglican Altruism on a Barbados Plantation, 1710–1834*, ed. Frank J. Klingberg, 3–14. Berkeley, Calif., 1949.

Knollenberg, Bernhard. *George Washington: The Virginia Period, 1732–1775.* Durham, N.C., 1964.

Levy, Philip. *George Washington Written Upon the Land: Nature, Memory, Myth, & Landscape.* Morgantown, W.Va., 2015

———. *Where the Cherry Tree Grew: The Story of Ferry Farm, George Washington's Boyhood Home.* New York, 2013.

Ligon, Richard. *A True & Exact History Of the Island of Barbadoes. Illustrated with a Map of the Island, as also the Principal Trees and Plants there, set forth in their due Proportions and Shapes, drawn out by their several and respective Scales. . . .* 1657; reprint, London, 1673.

Mazyck, Walter H. *George Washington and the Negro.* Washington, D.C., 1932.

McCulloch, Samuel Clyde, and John A. Schutz. "Of the Noble and Generous Benefaction of General Christopher Codrington." In *Codrington Chronicle: An Experiment in Anglican Altruism on a Barbados Plantation, 1710–1834,* ed. Frank J. Klingberg, 15–26. Berkeley, Calif., 1949.

Molen, Patricia A. "Population and Social Patterns in Barbados in the Early Eighteenth Century." *William and Mary Quarterly,* 3rd ser., 28 (1971): 287–300.

Moore, John Hamilton. *The New Practical Navigator; being an Epitome of Navigation, Rendered Easy To Any Common Capacity: containing all the Requisite Tables for Determining the Latitude and Longitude, and Keeping A Complete Reckoning at Sea: illustrated by Proper Rules and Examples, the whole exemplified in a Journal kept from England to the Island of Teneriffe. So That This Book, and the Nautical Almanac, Will Be Found Fully Sufficient for the Seaman and Teacher's Use. Constructed on a New Plan.* London, 1793.

Moxham, Robert Morgan. *Early Colonial Churches of Northern Virginia.* North Springfield, Va., 1974.

Neill, Edward D. *The Fairfaxes of England and America in the Seventeenth and Eighteenth Centuries, Including Letters from and to Hon. William Fairfax, President of Council of Virginia, and His Sons Col. George William Fairfax and Rev. Bryan, Eighth Lord Fairfax, the Neighbors and Friends of George Washington.* Albany, 1868.

Original Papers Relating to the Expedition to Carthagena. London, 1744.

Osborne, J. A. *Williamsburg in Colonial Times: Incidents in the Lives of the English Colonists in Virginia during the 17th and 18th centuries as revealed in old documents and files of* The Virginia Gazette. Richmond, 1935.

Palmer, Aaron J. *A Rule of Law: Elite Political Authority and the Coming of the Revolution in the South Carolina Lowcountry, 1763–1776.* Early American History Series: The American Colonies, 1500–1830, vol. 3. Leiden, Netherlands, 2014.

Pinckard, George. *Notes on the West Indies: written during the Expedition under the Command of the late General Sir Ralph Abercromby: including observations on The Island of Barbadoes . . . .* 3 vols. London, 1806.

Poole, R[obert]. *The Beneficent Bee: or, Traveller's Companion. Containing Each Day's Observation, in a Voyage from London, to Gibraltar, Barbadoes, Antigua, Barbuda, Mountserat, Nevis, St. Christopher's, St. Eustatia, Guardalupe, Virgin-Guada, Tortola, Santa Cruze, &c. Containing a summary Account of the said Places, their Inhabitants, Product, Money, Customs, &c. Interspersed with many useful Observations, and occasional Remarks. Calculated for the Benefit of such whose Business calls them to those Parts, or whose Curiosity inclines them to be acquainted therewith.* London, 1753.

Sailing Directions for the East-India or Oriental Pilot, for the Navigation between England and the Cape of Good Hope. London, 1781.

Schomburgk, Robert H. *The History of Barbados; Comprising A Geographical and Statistical Description of the Island; A Sketch of the Historical Events Since the Settlement; and an Account of Its Geology and Natural Productions.* London, 1848.

Seller, John. *Practical Navigation; or an Introduction to the Whole Art, containing The Doctrine of Plain and Spherical Triangles. Plain, Mercator, Great Circle Sailing; and Astronomical Problems. The Use of divers Instruments; as also of the Plain Chart, Mercator's Chart, and both Globes. Sundry Useful Tables in Navigation: And a Table of 10000 Logarithms, and of the Logarithm Sines, Tangents, and Secants.* London, 1711.

Smith, Frederick H., and Karl Watson. "Urbanity, Sociability, and Commercial Exchange in the Barbados Sugar Trade: A Comparative Colonial Archaeological Perspective on Bridgetown, Barbados in the Seventeenth Century." *International Journal of Historical Archaeology* 13 (2009): 63–79.

SPARKS, JARED, ed. *The Writings of George Washington; Being His Correspondence, Addresses, Messages, and Other Papers, Official and Private, Selected and Published from the Original Manuscripts.* 12 vols. Boston, 1833–37.

STEEL, DAVID. *The Elements and Practice of Rigging and Seamanship.* 2 vols. London, 1794.

TONER, J. M., ed. *The Daily Journal of Major George Washington, in 1751–2, Kept while on a Tour from Virginia to the Island of Barbadoes, with his invalid Brother, Maj. Lawrence Washington, Proprietor of Mount Vernon on the Potomac.* Albany, 1892.

TRUXTUN, THOMAS. *Remarks, Instructions, and Examples relating to the Latitude & Longitude; also, The Variation of the Compass . . .* Philadelphia, 1794.

WALKER, RALPH. *A Treatise on Magnetism, with a Description and Explanation of a Meridional and Azimuth Compass, for ascertaining the Quantity of Variation, without any calculation whatever, at any time of the day. Also Improvements upon Compasses in General, with Tables of Variation, for All Latitudes and Longitudes.* London, 1794.

WALTER, JAMES. *Memorials of Washington and of Mary, His Mother, and Martha, His Wife, From Letters and Papers of Robert Cary and James Sharples.* New York, 1887.

WARREN, JACK D., JR. "The Childhood of George Washington." *Northern Neck of Virginia Historical Magazine* 49 (1999): 5785–809.

WATSON, KARL. *The Civilised Island, Barbados: A Social History 1750–1816.* Barbados, 1979.

ZAGARRI, ROSEMARIE, ed. *David Humphreys' "Life of General Washington" with George Washington's "Remarks."* Athens, Ga., 1991.

INDEX

Italicized page numbers refer to illustrations. See Appendix A for "Glossary of Nautical Terms."

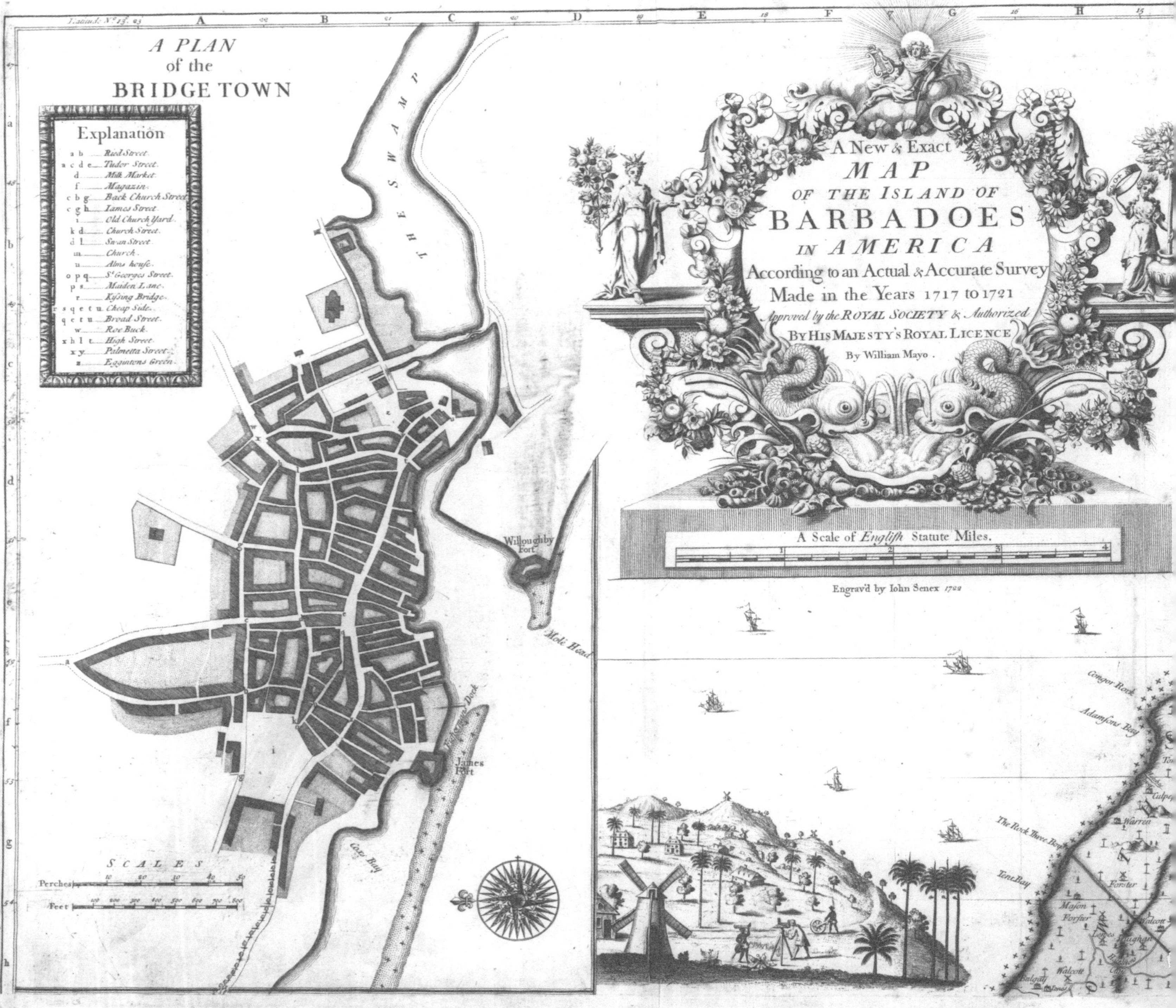

A PLAN
of the
BRIDGE TOWN
Explanation
a b ... Ried Street.
a c d e ... Tudor Street.
d ... Milk Market.
f ... Magazin.
c b g ... Back Church Street
c g h ... James Street.
i ... Old Church Yard.
k d ... Church Street.
d l ... Swan Street.
m ... Church.
n ... Alms house.
o p q ... St Georges Street.
p s ... Maiden Lane.
r ... Kissing Bridge.
r s q e t u ... Cheap Side.
q e t u ... Broad Street.
w ... Roe Buck.
x h l t ... High Street.
x y ... Palmetta Street.
z ... Egginton's Green.
THE SWAMP
Willoughby Fort
Mole Head
James Fort
SCALES
Perches
Feet
A New & Exact
MAP
OF THE ISLAND OF
BARBADOES
IN AMERICA
According to an Actual & Accurate Survey
Made in the Years 1717 to 1721
Approved by the ROYAL SOCIETY & Authorized
BY HIS MAJESTY'S ROYAL LICENCE
By William Mayo.
A Scale of English Statute Miles.
Engrav'd by Iohn Senex 1722
Congor Rock
Adamsons Bay
The Rock Three Boy
Tent Bay
Warren
Forster
Walcott